Oxford English for
Electronics

Eric H. Glendinning
John McEwan

Oxford University Press

Oxford University Press
Walton Street, Oxford OX2 6DP
Oxford New York
Athens Auckland Bangkok Bombay
Calcutta Cape Town Dar es Salaam Delhi
Florence Hong Kong Istanbul Karachi
Kuala Lumpur Madras Madrid Melbourne
Mexico City Nairobi Paris Singapore
Taipei Tokyo Toronto

and associated companies in
Berlin Ibadan

Oxford and *Oxford English* are trade marks of
Oxford University Press.

ISBN 0 19 457384 2
© Oxford University Press 1993

First published 1993
Fourth impression 1996

No unauthorized photocopying

All rights reserved. No part of this publication may
be reproduced, stored in a retrieval system, or
transmitted, in any form or by any means, electronic,
mechanical, photocopying, recording, or otherwise,
without the prior written permission of Oxford
University Press.

This book is sold subject to the condition that it shall
not, by way of trade or otherwise, be lent, resold,
hired out, or otherwise circulated without the
publisher's prior consent in any form of binding or
cover other than that in which it is published and
without a similar condition including this condition
being imposed on the subsequent purchaser.

The publisher and authors of *Oxford English for
Computing* and *Oxford English for Electronics* would
like to thank the teachers and students of the
following institutions for their advice and assistance
in the preparation of these books:

Italy
Istituti Tecnici Industriali:
  Aldini-Valeriani, Bologna
  Belluzi, Bologna
  Benedetto Castelli, Brescia
  Conti, Milan
  Fermi, Rome
  Fermi, Naples
  Gastaldi, Genoa
  Giordani, Naples
  Giorgi, Milan
  Giorgi, Rome
  Leonardo da Vinci, Florence
  Marconi, Verona
  Miano, San Giorgio, Naples
  Paeocapa, Bergamo
  Panetti, Bari
  Pasolini, Milan
  Peano, Turin
  San Felipo Neri, Rome
  Zuccante, Mestre
Istituti Professionali:
  Caselli, Siena
  Cinnici, Florence
  Galileo Galilei, Turin
  Galvani, Milan
Istituto Tecnico Commerciale Lorgna, Verona

France
Ecole Nationale du Commerce, Paris
Lycée Bouchardon, Chaumont
Lycée Monge, Chambery
Lycée du Dauphiné, Romans
Lycée Téchnologique Industriel, Valence
The publisher and authors would like to thank the
following for their kind permission to use articles,
extracts, or adaptations from copyright material. There
are instances where we have been unable to trace
or contact the copyright holder before our printing
deadline. We apologize for this apparent negligence.
If notified, the publisher will be pleased to rectify any
errors or omissions at the earliest opportunity.

Argus Publications, for diverse diagrams from
  Electronics Today and *Electronics Digest*;
M.W. Brimicombe, *Introducing Electronic Systems*,
  Thomas Nelson & Sons Ltd, 1987;
Channel 4 Support Services, for VHS Video recorder
  mechanism diagram;
T. Duncan, *Electronics for Today and Tomorrow* and
  Success in Electronics, John Murray (Publishers) Ltd;
Graphic News, for 'Making a record' and 'Digital
  watch' diagrams;
Guardian Newspapers Ltd, for extracts from
  Education Guardian. © 1990–92;
HMSO–CSO, for extracts from *Social Trends*;
Line Technical Illustrations, for 'Sound recording'
  diagram;
Maplin Electronics, *Electronics – The Maplin Magazine*;
Meridian – Communication by design, for 'High-
  definition TV', 'Loudspeaker', and 'Metal Detector'
  illustrations;
Stanley Thornes Publishers, *Steps in Electronics*;
Stevenson College, Edinburgh, questionnaire;
University of Strathclyde, brochure;
Wimborne Publishing Ltd, for extracts and diagrams
  from *Everyday Electronics Monthly Magazine*.

The publishers would like to thank the following for
their permission to reproduce photographs:

Argos; Barnaby's Picture Library; Creda Ltd; Robert
Ellis; Rob Judges; JVC (UK) Ltd; Life File (Emma Lee);
Redferns (MikeHutson); The Science Photo Library:
Martin Bond; Dr. Tony Brain; Ray Ellis; Simon Fraser;
G.E. Astro Space; Jerrican Ivaldi; Pat and Tom Leeson;
Nelson Morris; David Parker; Philippe Plailly; John
Sanford; The Telegraph Colour Library; John
Walmsley.

Technical Illustrations by Oxford Illustrators

Studio Photography by Pat Downing

Typeset in Monotype Photina and Univers by
Tradespools Ltd, Frome, Somerset

Printed in Hong Kong

Contents

1 Electronics in the home

Tuning-in

Task 1
Make a list of things in your house which use electronics. Compare your list with that of another group.

Task 2
Find out the meaning of these abbreviations. You can use Appendix 1 on page 188 to help you.

   1 IC   **2** CD   **3** hi-fi

Reading *Reading for a purpose*

In your study and work, it is important to have a clear purpose when you read. At the start of most units in this book, you will find tasks to give you that purpose.

Task 3
Read quickly through the text on the next page. Tick [✓] any items mentioned in the list you made in Task 1.

Electronics in the home

Electronics began at the start of the twentieth century with the invention of the vacuum tube. The first devices for everyday use were radios, followed by televisions, record players, and tape recorders. These devices were large and used a lot of power.

5 The invention of the transistor in 1947 meant that much smaller, low-powered devices could be developed. A wide variety of electronic devices such as hi-fi units and portable radios became common in the home.

It was not until 1958 that microelectronics began with the
10 development of ICs (integrated circuits) on silicon chips. This led to a great increase in the use of electronics in everyday items. The introduction of the microprocessor allowed electronics to be used for the control of many common processes.

Microprocessors are now used to control many household items such
15 as automatic washing-machines, dishwashers, central heating systems, sewing machines, and food processors. Electronic timers are found in digital alarm clocks, water heaters, electric cookers, and microwave ovens. Telephones use electronics to provide automatic dialling and answerphone facilities. New entertainment devices have
20 been developed, such as video recorders and CD (compact disc) players.

In the future, electronics are likely to become even more common in the home as multimedia entertainment systems and computer-controlled robots are developed.

Task 4 Fill in the gaps in this table with the help of the text.

Date	Invention	Applications in the home
early 20th century	_____	_____
_____	transistor	_____
1958	_____	automatic washing-machines,
future	—	_____

Task 5 Use the space below to make a list of ways in which you think electronics may be used in the home in the future.

_____

_____

_____

_____

_____

_____

_____

_____

Reading *Understanding diagrams*

In electronics, you have to read not only texts, but also diagrams. You have to be able to combine information from both diagram and text. This text introduces two kinds of diagrams often used in electronics.

Task 6

Read the text below to find the answers to these questions:

1 What do we call the two types of diagrams shown in the text?
2 What do we call the approach to electronics which focuses on the function of units?

Understanding electronic diagrams

Although electronic devices may look complicated, they are made up of common basic units ('building blocks') connected together. The function of each of these units and the path of the signals between them can be shown in a block diagram. For example, the block
5 diagram of a simple radio is shown in Fig. 1.

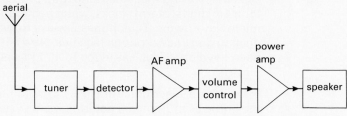

Fig. 1

To understand how the radio works, it is more important to understand the function of each unit than to know what components are used. This is known as a systems approach to electronics. For example, in Fig. 1 the tuner selects the required signal, the detector
10 then separates off the audio part of the signal, and the AF amplifier (amp) amplifies it.

The connections and values of the components inside these basic units can be shown in a circuit diagram using standard electronic symbols. Fig. 2 shows the circuit diagram for the simple radio.

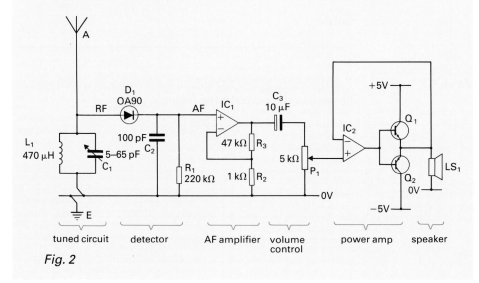

Fig. 2

Task 7

How many of the circuit symbols in Fig. 2 can you identify? Use Appendix 2 on page 206 to help you.

Language study *Describing block diagrams and circuits*

Look again at Fig. 1 above. We can describe it like this:

The radio | **consists of** | *a tuner, a detector, and an AF amplifier.*
| **is composed of** |

Using *comprise*, we can start our description with the blocks:

A tuner, a detector, and an AF amplifier | **comprise** | *the radio.*

We can describe the links between each building block using these expressions:

The tuner | **is connected to** | *the detector.*
| **is linked to** |

Look again at Fig. 2. We can describe the values of the components like this:

R1   *a two-hundred-and-twenty-kilohm resistor*
C2   *a hundred-picofarad (puff) capacitor*

Task 8

Describe the value of these components:

1   R2
2   C1
3   R3
4   C3
5   P1
6   L1

This table provides the terms you need.

Prefix	Symbol	Multiple	Example	
giga	G	10^9	GHz	gigahertz
mega	M	10^6	MΩ	megohms
kilo	k	10^3	kV	kilovolts
deci	d	10^{-1}	dB	decibels
milli	m	10^{-3}	mW	milliwatts
micro	μ	10^{-6}	μH	microhenries
nano	n	10^{-9}	nF	nanofarads
pico	p	10^{-12}	pF	picofarads

Looking now at the basic units of the circuit, we can describe the volume control like this:

> The volume control consists of a ten-microfarad electrolytic capacitor connected in series with a five-kilohm potentiometer (pot). The positive terminal of the capacitor is connected to the output of the AF amplifier and the wiper of the pot is connected to the power amp. The
> 5   third terminal of the pot is connected to the zero voltage supply rail, which is earthed.

Fill in the gaps in this description of the tuned circuit shown in Fig. 2. Each gap represents one word.

The circuit ^{1}_____ of a four hundred and seventy ^{2}_____ inductor which is connected in parallel with a ^{3}_____ capacitor. The ^{4}_____ can be varied between five and sixty-five ^{5}_____ . The aerial is ^{6}_____ to the top end of the tuner. It is also connected to the positive terminal of the ^{7}_____ in the detector. The bottom end of the tuner is connected to earth via the zero voltage ^{8}_____ rail.

Speaking practice

Work in pairs, **A** and **B**. Complete your circuit diagram with help from your partner.

Ask questions like these:

> *What kind of component is P1?*
> *What's the value of C1?*
> *What is connected between the collector of Q2 and the positive side of the battery?*

If you don't understand your partner, say:

> *I'm sorry, I don't understand. Could you say that again, please?*
> *Could you speak more slowly?*

If your partner doesn't understand you at first, try phrasing your answer in a different way. For example:

> *It's a variable resistor. It's a resistor which you can vary or change by turning the control. It's called a variable resistor.*

Student A: Your circuit diagram is on page 174.
Student B: Your circuit diagram is on page 181.

Writing *Describing diagrams*

With the help of the diagram, fill in the gaps in the description on page 12. Each gap represents one word. The description should answer these questions:

1 What is the diagram of?
2 What does it consist of in terms of blocks?
3 How are the blocks connected?
4 What is the function of each block?

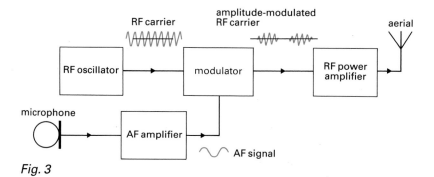

Fig. 3

Fig. 3 shows the block diagram of an amplitude-modulated (AM) radio transmitter. It [1]_____ of a radio frequency (RF) oscillator, a [2]_____, an audio frequency (AF) amplifier, and an RF power amplifier. The RF [3]_____ generates an RF [4]_____ wave which is fed into the modulator.

The microphone converts sounds into audio frequency signals which are amplified by the AF [5]_____. The modulator then uses the amplified AF [6]_____ to modulate the RF carrier wave.

The power of the modulated carrier wave is increased by the RF [7]_____ amplifier. The strong modulated output signals are fed to the [8]_____ which enables them to be transmitted over long distances.

2 Choosing a course

Reading *Guessing from context*

You will not understand every word you read. Often you will have to guess the meaning of an unfamiliar word using both your knowledge of English and your knowledge of the world. The text which follows practises guessing from context. The topic is 'Studying electronics in the UK'.

Task 1

Fill in the gaps in this text. Each gap represents one word. Compare your answers with your partner. More than one answer is possible for many of the gaps.

In the United Kingdom, you [1]_____ study electronics at a college of further education or a university.

A college of further education will [2]_____ students who have completed a minimum of four years [3]_____ secondary school. Most students study full-time [4]_____ colleges also offer day release classes [5]_____ people employed by local businesses who are given time [6]_____ work to attend courses. Colleges also provide evening [7]_____ for full-time workers and members of the local community [8]_____ want to study in their spare time.

14

Most university students will have completed six years of

secondary [9]_____ . Some will have completed four years and

[10]_____ taken a course at a college of further education.

From a college you can [11]_____ a certificate or diploma. A diploma

usually requires a longer period of study [12]_____ a certificate.

Universities give degrees. A Bachelor's degree takes three to

four years of [13]_____ . A Master's degree usually requires a further

[14]_____

Task 2   Listen to the text and note the words used on the tape for each gap.

Task 3   Find out the courses your local college or institute offers in information technology. List them and try to translate the course titles into English.

Task 4   Study this list of courses. Do any match the courses offered by your local college?

Course Guide
Information Technology

The following programmes are offered by Information Technology:

Code	Course Title
IT 1	Full-time National Certificate Course for Women in Electronics
IT 2	Full-time National Certificate Course in Information Technology
IT 3	Day release National Certificate in Information Technology
IT 4	Day release National Certificate in Electronics
IT 5	National Certificate evening classes in Electronics
IT 7	National Certificate evening classes in Electronics and Computers in Music
IT 8	Autocad for Industry
IT 9	Evening classes in Autocad

Further information may be obtained on course provision by contacting the College Information Centre and requesting the appropriate course leaflet by code number.

Information Centre
Stevenson College
Bankhead Avenue
Sighthill
Edinburgh EH11 4DE

Telephone 031-453-2761

Which course would best meet the needs of these people? Answer using the course code. Compare answers with another student.

1 A school leaver who wants a qualification in information technology.
2 A worker in a company which makes electronic instruments and which is willing to give employees time off each week to attend a course which would help their career.
3 A worker in an engineering company who wants to find a new job in the electronics industry.
4 A manager who wants to train a small group of technicians in computer-aided design (CAD).
5 A housewife who wants to go back to work and would like a job in the electronics industry.
6 A rock musician who wants to create new sounds.

Task 6

Study this information about two courses in electronics. Find three similarities and three differences between these courses.

Course 1
Introduction to Electronic Systems

Description	This course provides a basic introduction to the world of electronic systems for the complete beginner. It illustrates how real-life problems can be solved by electronic means.
Award	National Certificate
College	Bankhead
Mode	Evening
Duration	16 weeks x 2½ hours

Course 2
National Certificate in Information Technology

Description	A two-year programme of electronics, control systems, and technical computing modules for technicians in employment.
Award	National Certificate
College	Bankhead
Mode	Day release
Duration	2 years of 39 weeks per year

Language study   *Comparison and contrast, 1*

We can describe similarities like this:

1 ***Both** courses are provided by Bankhead College.*
2 ***Like** Course 1, Course 2 deals with electronics.*
3 *Course 2 **is similar to** Course 1 in that it deals with electronics.*

We can describe differences like this:

4 *Course 2 is much long**er than** Course 1.*
5 *Course 2 is day release **but** Course 1 is an evening course.*
6 *Course 1 is for complete beginners **whereas** Course 2 is for technicians.*

Task 7   Study the course descriptions below of two higher level qualifications. Complete this table of differences between the courses.

	BTech	HND
Duration	3 years	
Award		Diploma
Institutes	Strathclyde and Bell	
Main subjects (unique)	electromagnetism, foreign language, engineering management, signals and systems,	quality management
Options (unique)	optoelectronics, signal processing	

Bachelor of Technology (BTech) in Electrical and Electronic Engineering

Duration
Three years full-time

The Course

The degree resulting from this joint course between Strathclyde University and Bell College is awarded by Strathclyde University. Over the three years, students spend about half of the course in each institution. The BTech is a balance of theory and practical skills. It will enable graduates to attain the status of Incorporated Engineer after a period of industrial training and experience. It bridges the gap between HND and BEng Honours courses and there are transfer routes possible between all these courses.

Subjects

First Year – Mathematics; Electrotechnology; Digital and Computer Systems; Analogue Electronics; Software Engineering; Engineering Applications.

Second Year – Mathematics; Digital and Analogue Electronics; Electromagnetism; Power Engineering; Microprocessor Applications; System Principles; Circuit Analysis; Electronic Design and Production; Foreign Language.

Third Year – Electrotechnology; Engineering Management; Signals and Systems; Software Development; Measurement and Control; Data Communications Project.

Students will also choose from a range of options including CAD, Optoelectronics, Materials, Power Plant, Signal Processing, and others.

Higher National Diploma in Electronic and Electrical Engineering

Duration
Two years full-time.

The Course

This is a new HND course, planned after market research among employers and former students. This research identified the kinds of jobs, equipment, and management skills which holders of an HND must have in addition to their technological abilities. From this information we were able to plan the most appropriate course content. All students will study a broad range of subjects before choosing the options which will best suit their intended career. The diploma is taught and awarded by Bell College.

Subjects

First Year – there will be a range of introductory subjects to help everyone become familiar with new subject areas. These will be followed by: Electrotechnology; Electronics; Computer Programming and Applications; Mathematics; Complementary Studies.

Second Year – Electrotechnology; Computer Programming; Quality Management; Computer Aided Design; Complementary Studies; Project; and a range of options covering electronics, power and machines, data communications, control systems, and electronic production.

Task 8   Using the completed table and the course descriptions, describe the similarities and differences between the courses.

Word study *Word stress*

Words are divided into syllables. For example:

> com.mu.ni.ca.tion

Each syllable is pronounced separately, but normally only one syllable is stressed. That means it is said more slowly and clearly than the other syllables.

The stressed syllable in *communication* is *ca*. A good dictionary divides the important words into syllables and shows the stressed syllable. For example:

> com.mu.ni.'ca.tion

Task 9 Listen to these words. Try to mark the stressed syllable.

1	college	**4**	diploma	**7**	management	**10**	technician
2	institute	**5**	information	**8**	engineering		
3	university	**6**	electronics	**9**	technical		

Writing *Requesting information*

In a formal letter, we can request information using expressions like these:

> *Please send me . . .*
> *I would be grateful if you could / would send me . . .*

Task 10 Write a letter to the college mentioned in Task 4 asking for a leaflet on a course which interests you. Your letter should be set out like this:

```
                                           21 Route de St Fargeau,
                                           18900 Russe,
                                           FRANCE.

                                           30 May 19__

        Information Centre,
        Baird College,
        Logie Street,
        PORTLAND LK4 3GF,
        UK.


        Dear Sir/Madam,

        Please send me further information on your
        Electronic Engineering Course, EE3 — Full-time
        National Certificate Course in Electronic
        Engineering.

        Yours faithfully,

        Daniel Romero

        DANIEL ROMERO
```

3   Full-time student

Listening

You are going to hear an interview with Alan, a Scottish student of electronics at a college of further education.

Task 1

Here is Alan's weekly timetable. Some of the information is missing. Before you listen, try to answer these questions about the timetable:

1. What time does Alan start in the morning?
2. What time does he finish for the day?
3. What do you think happens between 10.15 and 10.45?
4. What other time does this happen?
5. How often does he have maths?
6. When is the lunch break?

	Monday	Tuesday	Wednesday	Thursday	Friday
8.45–10.15	Electrical Principles	Analogue Electronics	Analogue Electronics	Electrical Principles	(5)
10.45–12.15	(1)	(2)	Communications	Computing	(6)
1.15–2.45	Maths	(3)	(4)	Maths	Maths
3.00–4.30	Programmable Systems	↓	↓	Programmable Systems	Digital Electronics

Task 2   ⌨   Now listen to the interview. Try to complete the information missing from the timetable. Compare answers with your partner.

Task 3 🖭 Listen to the tape again. Answer these questions:

1 Why did so many students drop out of Alan's course?
2 Why does he dislike Communications?
3 Why is it hard to use the indoor stadium?
4 Why is there a problem with his motorbike?

Writing *Comparing and contrasting, 1*

Task 4 Write your own timetable in English.

Monday	Tuesday	Wednesday	Thursday	Friday

Task 5 Now complete this table. Note any similarities and any differences between Alan's week and your own.

Alan's subjects	Hours per week	Your subjects	Hours per week
Maths	4.5		

Task 6 Write a short comparison and contrast of your timetable and Alan's using any of the ways in the Language study on page 16 to describe similarities and differences.

4 **Component values**

Technical reading *Resistor values*

Task 1 Fill in the missing colours in this table with the help of the text.

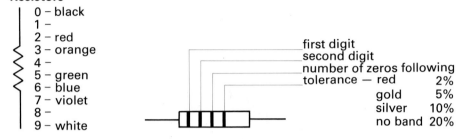

Resistors

```
  0 – black
  1 –
  2 – red
  3 – orange
  4 –
  5 – green
  6 – blue
  7 – violet
  8 –
  9 – white
```

first digit
second digit
number of zeros following
tolerance — red   2%
              gold   5%
              silver   10%
              no band 20%

Reading the resistor code

Resistors are coded with coloured bands to ease the problem of marking such small components.

The numbers corresponding to the ten colours used and the values per position are shown above.

5 For example, 180,000 ohms is coded with the first digit brown, then grey and finally yellow. The fourth band indicates the tolerance that the value has with respect to the stated value. For example, silver indicates 10% tolerance, meaning that the 180,000 ohms could vary between 180,000 ± 18,000, i.e. 162,000 to 198,000.

10 These tolerances may seem to reflect poor manufacture but in most circuits they are, in fact, quite satisfactory. Relaxing the tolerance enables the maker to sell them more cheaply.

Task 2 Find the values and tolerances of resistors banded as follows. Then compare your answers with your partner.

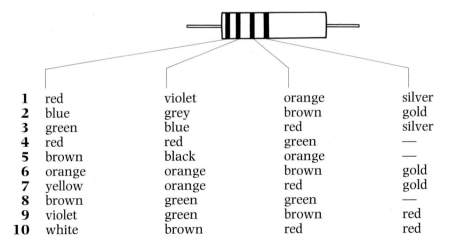

1	red	violet	orange	silver
2	blue	grey	brown	gold
3	green	blue	red	silver
4	red	red	green	—
5	brown	black	orange	—
6	orange	orange	brown	gold
7	yellow	orange	red	gold
8	brown	green	green	—
9	violet	green	brown	red
10	white	brown	red	red

Task 3

Read this additional text. Answer the questions below, which refer to both texts.

Preferred values

If the maker tried to produce and sell every value of resistance that exists, there would be chaos and the costs would be greatly increased. The actual values made,

5 therefore, are limited to a range called the preferred values. These are listed in the table.

The values may seem illogical at first sight, but this is not so. They stem from the fact

10 that the tolerance extremes of a value reach the extremes of adjacent values, thereby covering the whole range without overlap. Values normally available stop in the megohm decade.

Tolerance

±5%	±10%	±20%
1.0	1.0	1.0
1.1		
1.2	1.2	
1.5	1.5	1.5
1.6		
1.8	1.8	
2.0		
2.2	2.2	2.2
2.4		
2.7	2.7	
3.0		
3.3	3.3	3.3
3.6		
3.9	3.9	
4.3		
4.7	4.7	4.7
5.1		
5.6	5.6	
6.2		
6.8	6.8	6.8
7.5		
8.2		
9.1		

1 Why are resistors coded with coloured bands rather than some other form of marking?

2 What would be the effect of making resistors with a much higher tolerance?

3 Between which values might a resistor marked green, blue, orange, and silver vary?

4 Why do manufacturers make resistors in the preferred values shown rather than in equally stepped values?

Technical reading *Capacitor values*

Task 4

Use the following information to name the colour bandings of the capacitors below. (Note: 1nF = 1000pF). For example:

220pF, 2.5%

Band 1 red = 2   Band 3 brown = one zero
Band 2 red = 2   Band 4 orange = 2.5% tolerance

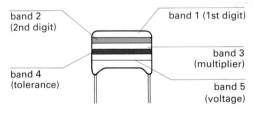

C280 capacitor colour coding. The first three bands give the value (in pF) using the same system as for the four band resistor coding.

		band	
		4	5
	black	20%	——
	white	10%	——
	green	5%	——
colour	orange	2.5%	——
	red	2%	250V
	brown	1%	——
	yellow	——	400V

1 100pF, 20%   3 22nF, 5% 250V
2 180pF, 10%   4 47nF, 20%

Technical reading *Diode codes*

Task 5 Identify these diodes with the help of the text below.

1 BAX16 **2** BY126 **3** BZX55C2V4 **4** AA119 **5** BPX65

Diode coding

The European system for classifying semiconductor diodes involves an alphanumeric code which employs either two letters and three figures (general purpose diodes) or three letters and two figures (special purpose diodes). The first two letters have the following
5 significance:

First letter – semiconductor material:

A germanium
B silicon
C gallium arsenide etc.
10 D photodiodes etc.

Second letter – application:

A general purpose diode
B tuning (varicap) diode
E tunnel diode
15 P photovoltaic diode
Q light-emitting diode
T controlled rectifier
X varactor diode
Y power rectifier
20 Z zener diode

In the case of diodes for specialized applications, the third letter does not generally have any particular significance. Zener diodes have an additional letter (which appears *after* the numbers) which denotes the tolerance of the zener voltage. The following letters are used:

25 A±1%
B±2%
C±5%
D±10%

Zener diodes also have additional characters which indicate the zener
30 voltage (e.g. 9V1 denotes 9.1V).

Example

Identify each of the following diodes:
(i) AA113
(ii) BB105
35 *(iii) BZY88C4V7*

Diode (i) is a general-purpose germanium diode.
Diode (ii) is a silicon diode for tuning applications (sometimes referred to as a varicap).
Diode (iii) is a silicon zener diode having 5% tolerance and 4.7V zener
40 voltage.

Writing *Linking facts and ideas, 1*

Study these statements about resistors:

1 *Resistors are electronic components.*
2 *Resistors are used to add resistance to a circuit.*

We can link the statements like this:

*Resistors are electronic components **which** add resistance to a circuit.*

which *add resistance to a circuit* is a relative clause. This clause helps to define resistors. It is an essential part of the sentence.

Study these statements.

3 *Very accurate resistors are used in instruments.*
4 *These resistors are expensive.*

We can link the statements like this:

*Very accurate resistors, **which** are expensive, are used in instruments.*

which *are expensive* is also a relative clause, but it contains information that is not essential to the sentence. Relative clauses that carry inessential information are separated from the rest of the sentence by commas.

Study these statements:

5 *Each resistor is marked with colours.*
6 *The colours indicate the value of the resistor.*

Statement 6 explains the purpose of the colours. We can link these statements like this:

*Each resistor is marked with colours **to indicate** its value.*

Task 6

Study this diagram of a carbon resistor and consider how it is made.

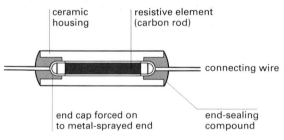

Now join the following groups of statements to make longer sentences. Use the words printed in *italics* above each group. You may omit words and make whatever changes you think are necessary in the word order and punctuation of the sentences.

1 *which*
A resistor is a component.
A resistor is used to add resistance to a circuit.

2 *which*
Carbon resistors are made of compressed graphite.
The graphite is formed into small tubes.

3 *to*
A ceramic coating is applied over the graphite.
The ceramic coating insulates the graphite.

4 *to*

The ends of the graphite are sprayed with metal.
This forms contacts.

5 *which*

End caps are forced on the metal-sprayed ends.
The caps have connecting wires attached.

6 *to*

The ceramic is marked with colour bands.
The bands indicate the value and tolerance.

7 *which*

Resistors are made in a range of preferred values.
These values meet all the needs of circuit designers.

5 Batteries

Tuning-in

Task 1

Study this statement:

Twenty billion batteries are sold every year.

Why do you think this is so? What different kinds of batteries are there? List some of the things you use which contain batteries. Compare your list with someone else's.

Task 2

Try to complete this table of the differences between two kinds of cells. Use these terms:

secondary	manganese dioxide	cadmium	primary
nickel	zinc	portable phones	torches

	Zinc-carbon cell	**NiCad cell**
Type of cell		
Positive electrode		
Negative electrode		
Example of use		

Task 3

Now listen to the tape to check your answers.

Now read this text. Note any further information about these cells.

	Zinc-carbon cell	**NiCad cell**
Electrolyte		
EMF		

Zinc-carbon cell

It has a zinc negative electrode, a manganese dioxide positive electrode, and the electrolyte is a solution of ammonium chloride. The carbon rod is in contact with the positive electrode (but is not involved in the chemical reaction) and is called the current collector. The EMF is

5 1.5V and the internal resistance about 0.5Ω. This is the most popular cell for low-current or occasional use, e.g. in torches.

Nickel-cadmium cell (NiCad)

The electrodes are of nickel (+) and cadmium (–) and the electrolyte is potassium hydroxide. It has an EMF of 1.2V and is made in the same sizes as primary cells, e.g. HP2, PP3; button types are also available.

10 High currents can be supplied. Recharging must be by a constant current power supply because of the very low internal resistance.

Task 5

Label this diagram of a Zinc-carbon cell with these terms. More than one term can refer to the same part of the diagram.

a zinc can
b current collector
c jacket
d carbon rod
e positive electrode
f electrolyte

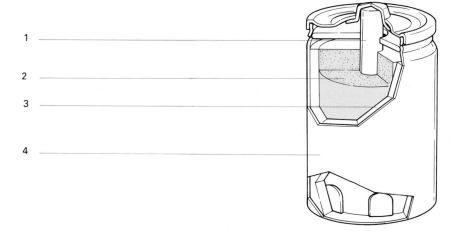

Language study *Describing components*

Two questions we may need to answer when we describe components are:

1 What is it called?
2 What does it do?

In other words, we need to be able to:

1 label components.
2 describe their function.

We can use these ways of labelling components:

It **is called** a Zinc-carbon cell.
It **is known as** a NiCad cell.

We can describe the function of components like this:

A cell **provides** electricity.
Cells **change** chemical energy into electricity.

Task 6

Here are some circuit symbols. Label them and describe their function. For example:

5 h *It's called a transformer. It steps AC voltages up or down.*

This list of functions may help you.

a	varies capacitance in a circuit	**f**	protects a circuit
b	rectifies alternating current	**g**	varies the current in a circuit
c	adds resistance to a circuit	**h**	steps AC voltages up or down
d	measures very small currents	**i**	receives RF signals
e	breaks a circuit	**j**	measures voltages

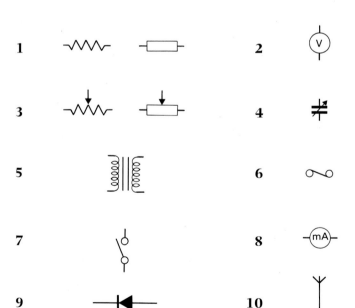

Speaking practice

Task 7

Work in pairs, **A** and **B**. You have some details, but not all, about two kinds of cells. Find out the missing details from your neighbour so that you can complete your table.

Student A: Your table is on page 174.
Student B: Your table is on page 181.

Word study *Verbs and related nouns*

Task 8

Each of these verbs has a related noun ending in *-er* or *-or* which refers to an instrument or component. Complete the column of nouns. You have met these nouns in this and earlier units.

	Verb	**Noun**
Example	*record*	*recorder*
1	oscillate	_____
2	transmit	_____
3	transform	_____
4	charge	_____
5	rectify	_____
6	process	_____
7	amplify	_____
8	collect	_____
9	detect	_____
10	tune	_____

Technical reading *Battery charger*

Task 9

Study this circuit diagram of a battery charger and try to name all the components.

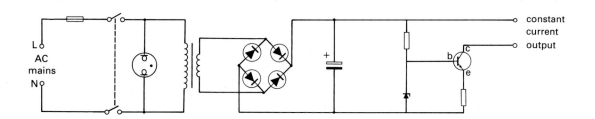

29

Now read this text to check your answers:

The power to drive an electronic circuit is normally provided by an AC mains power supply but batteries are often used for portable equipment. Secondary cells can be recharged to their original voltage and can therefore be used many times over.

5 Recharging is done using a battery charger which consists of a mains power supply with a DC output slightly larger than the required battery EMF. A current is driven through the battery in the opposite direction to its normal output current. The block diagram of a battery charger is shown in Fig. 1.

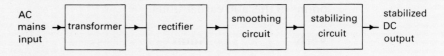

Fig. 1

10 The first stage consists of a transformer which steps down the voltage of the AC mains (see Fig. 2).

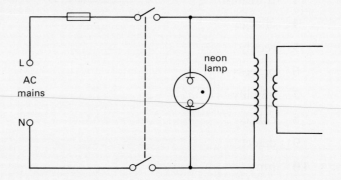

Fig. 2

The charger is switched on and off by a double-pole switch connected in series with the mains input. A neon lamp, connected across the primary of the transformer, shows when the charger is on. A fuse is
15 connected in the live side of the supply to protect the transformer.

The second stage is a bridge rectifier which converts the AC voltage to a DC voltage (see Fig. 3).

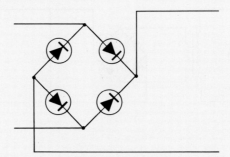

Fig. 3

This can be made from discrete components but more usually consists of four diodes contained in one package. It is mounted on an
20 aluminium heatsink to keep the diodes from overheating.

The third stage is a smoothing circuit. It removes the fluctuations in the DC output of the rectifier. It consists of a large electrolytic capacitor connected in parallel with the rectifier as shown in Fig. 4.

Fig. 4

The final stage is a stabilizing circuit consisting of a transistor biased
25 by two resistors and a zener diode. This prevents the output from changing when the load varies. NiCad batteries have such a small internal resistance that the charger must produce a constant current output (see Fig. 5).

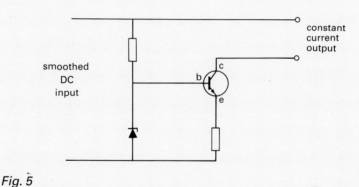

Fig. 5

Task 10

Match each component or unit with its function in a battery charger. For example:

The transformer steps down the AC mains voltage.

Component/Unit		Function in a battery charger	
1	transformer	**a**	steps down the AC mains voltage
2	double-pole switch	**b**	prevents the output from changing when the load varies
3	neon lamp		
4	fuse	**c**	keeps the diodes from overheating
5	rectifier	**d**	shows when the charger is on
6	aluminium heatsink	**e**	removes the fluctuations in the DC output of the rectifier
7	smoothing circuit		
8	stabilizing circuit	**f**	protects the transformer
		g	converts the AC voltage to a DC voltage
		h	switches the charger on and off

Writing *Describing diagrams*

One way of planning your writing is to think of questions which your readers will want to know the answers to. In the task which follows, base your description on the questions set for you.

Task 11

Describe the block diagram of the battery charger and the function of each building block. Your description should answer these questions:

1 What is the function of a battery charger?
2 What does it consist of in terms of blocks?
3 How are the blocks connected?
4 What is the function of each block?

6 Making a recording

Tuning-in

Task 1
Study this diagram. It shows the stages in making a recording. Try to match the short texts which follow to each stage. Compare your answers with your partner.

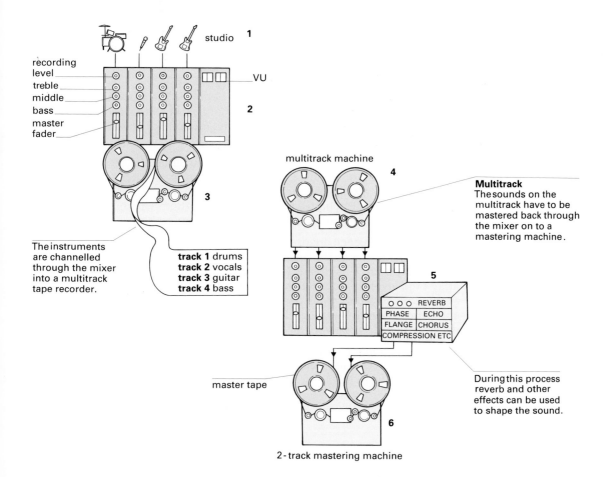

Multitrack
The sounds on the multitrack have to be mastered back through the mixer on to a mastering machine.

The instruments are channelled through the mixer into a multitrack tape recorder.

track 1 drums
track 2 vocals
track 3 guitar
track 4 bass

During this process reverb and other effects can be used to shape the sound.

2-track mastering machine

a Each microphone input is mixed on a mixer. In a commercial recording studio this is done by a sound engineer.
b The sounds on the multitrack are remixed until the musicians are happy with the sound.
c The output is recorded on a two-track mastering machine. The product is a master tape with two stereo channels.
d The musicians play in a recording studio. Each voice and instrument is recorded using different microphones.
e The instruments are channelled through the mixer into a multitrack tape recorder.
f During this process, effects, such as reverb, are used to shape the sound.

Read this text to check your answers.

Making a recording

For professional recording, the process begins in the studio. Each vocalist, instrument, or group of instruments is linked to a microphone. Each microphone is plugged into one of up to 72 channels on a mixer or mixing desk.

5 The mixing desk allows the studio engineer to adjust the recording level for each channel. This is shown by a VU meter or a bargraph where the indicator is a sequence of lights. Too low a level results in background hiss; too high a level causes distortion. The mixer also has EQ (equalization) controls which adjust bass and treble.

10 The output from each channel is fed to a track on a multitrack tape recorder. After the music has been recorded on the multitrack, it is mastered down. This means that it is fed back through the mixer to adjust the levels of vocalist and instruments in relation to each other. At this time, effects can be used to alter the sound. One of the most

15 common is reverb (reverberation) which can make the music sound as if it was recorded in a very large building or a very small room.

The edited sound is recorded on a two-track mastering machine to produce a master tape. The master is then used to make records, cassettes, CDs, or MDs.

Language study *Describing a process*

In English, the passive is often used to describe processes. Study these examples:

1 *Each instrument **is recorded**.*
2 *Special effects **are used**.*
3 *Copies can **be made**.*

The passive is made using the verb *to be* (*be, is, are,* etc.) and the past participle of the verb. Most technical verbs are regular so the past participle is made simply by adding *-ed* (Example 1). Watch the spelling of the past participle of verbs like *control* (*controlled*) and *use* (Example 2). The passive infinitive is used in the same place as ordinary infinitives, for example after verbs like *must* and *can* (Example 3).

Task 3

Complete this summary of how to make a recording, by putting each of the verbs in brackets in the correct form. For example:

> Each instrument (record) using a microphone.
> *Each instrument **is recorded** using a microphone.*

Each instrument ¹_____ (record) using a microphone. The sound ²_____ (feed) to a mixing desk. The recording level ³_____ (control) and the EQ ⁴_____ (adjust) by the sound engineer. The output ⁵_____ (record) on a multitrack. The sounds from the multitrack ⁶_____ (master) back through the mixer. The tape ⁷_____ (remix) until the musicians are happy with the sound. Special effects can ⁸_____ (add) on the mixing desk. The remixed tape ⁹_____ (master down) to produce a master tape. This can ¹⁰_____ (use) to produce copies in many different formats.

Task 4

Listen to the *-ed* form of these verbs. Write the verbs in the correct column according to the sound of their *-ed* ending.

record   check   adjust   remix   shape   add
use   produce   control   master   play

	1 /ɪd/	**2** /d/	**3** /t/
Examples:	*add*	*use*	*shape*

Word study   *Topic sets, 1*

One way of remembering new words is to group them into topic sets according to their area of meaning. The words in Task 5 are all concerned with making a recording. They fall into three topic sets: people, places, and equipment. Make your own topic sets for other units in this book.

Task 5

Write these words in the correct column:

studio   sound engineer   microphone   multitrack recorder
mixer   vocalist   musician   master tape

Making a recording

Places	**People**	**Equipment**
_____	_____	_____
_____	_____	_____
_____	_____	_____
_____	_____	_____

Writing *Describing a process*

There are many stages involved in the production of CD discs. The more important ones are shown in Fig. 1.

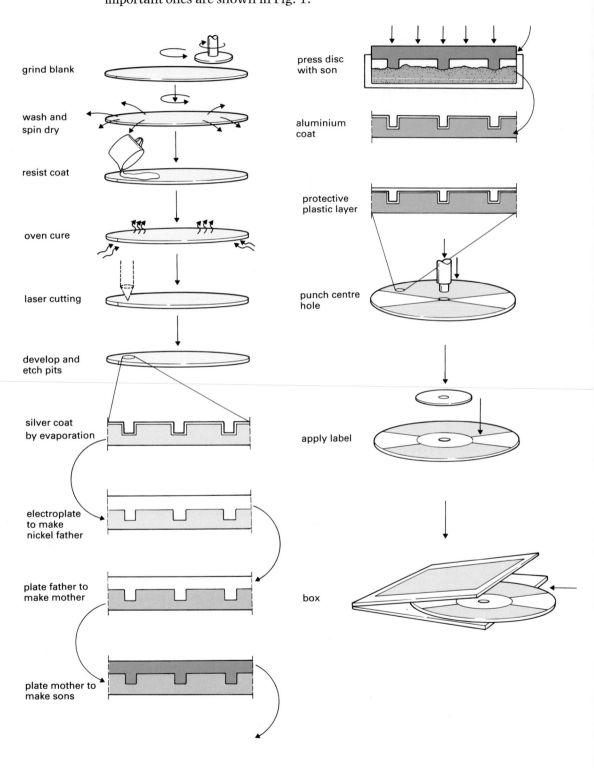

grind blank

wash and spin dry

resist coat

oven cure

laser cutting

develop and etch pits

silver coat by evaporation

electroplate to make nickel father

plate father to make mother

plate mother to make sons

press disc with son

aluminium coat

protective plastic layer

punch centre hole

apply label

box

Fig. 1

With the help of the diagram opposite, complete the gaps in this description of the process. Each gap requires one word.

Firstly, a blank perspex disc is [1]_____ and polished to optical flatness. Next, it is [2]_____ and spin-dried. It is then [3]_____ with a thin layer of photoresist and cured in an [4]_____. After that, as the disc is revolved, a [5]_____ beam is used to mark the audio information pattern on its surface. This process is [6]_____ as 'cutting' the disc. The photoresist is then developed and [7]_____ to produce [8]_____ in the disc's surface. These pits represent the digital audio pattern.

The disc is then given a thin [9]_____ coat to make it electrically conductive. Next, electroplating is used to make a series of positive and [10]_____ copies of the master disc. The final negative copy is used to [11]_____ a large number of identical CDs. The surface of the CD containing the pit marks is then [12]_____ with a 10mm layer of [13]_____ followed by a protective layer of [14]_____. After [15]_____ the centre hole, a [16]_____ is applied and the CD is packaged.

7 Sound engineer

Listening

Steve is a sound engineer. He describes his work and how you can make your own recordings of live music. The recording is in two parts:

Part 1   The job
Part 2   Making your own recording

Task 1

Before you listen, try to match these specialist terms to their definitions. Compare your answers with your partner.

1   compression
2   distortion
3   echo
4   reverb

a   A complete unit of sound of any length is repeated.
b   What happens to sound when the signal is too high.
c   Weak signals are boosted and strong signals reduced so that the sound is compressed into a more easily recordable range.
d   Sound is reproduced in such a way that listeners feel they are in a room of a particular size.

Task 2

As you listen to Part 1, answer these questions:

1   Where does Steve work?
    a   college
    b   commercial radio station
    c   recording studio
    d   mobile disco

2   Where did he work previously?
   a   college
   b   commercial radio station
   c   recording studio
   d   mobile disco

3   When he was a school and college student, what interest did he have in sound?
   a   he had his own band
   b   he had his own mobile disco
   c   he used to make commercials
   d   he recorded live music

4   What was he recording that day?
   a   a Japanese radio programme
   b   a tape compilation
   c   a self-study language tape
   d   a whisky commercial

Task 3   As you listen to Part 2, answer these questions:

1   Which one of these is *not* required to make a recording?
   a   a mike
   b   a tape recorder
   c   a recording studio
   d   a room with good acoustics

2   What will allow you to make a proper recording?
   a   a Portastudio
   b   a VU meter
   c   a bargraph
   d   special effects

3   What does a Portastudio combine?
   a   special effects and a cassette deck
   b   a mike and a cassette deck
   c   a mixer and a cassette deck
   d   a VU meter and a cassette deck

4   Which one of the following is *not* a special effect?
   a   reverb
   b   echo
   c   compression
   d   distortion

5   What should you do before making the final copy?
   a   take a break
   b   check the recording levels
   c   add special effects
   d   run the tape backwards

Task 4   Listen again to the complete interview and answer these more difficult questions:

1   What was unusual about the recording made that day?
2   What's the difference between a commercial mixing desk and a Portastudio?
3   Why should you keep an eye on the bargraph or VU meter when recording?
4   How is mixing down like developing and printing a photograph?
5   What's the danger of mixing down without a break?

Reading *Comparing sources*

In work and study we depend on information from different sources, for example, what we hear from lecturers and what we read in textbooks. In the exercise that follows, you are asked to compare a listening text and a reading text.

Task 5

Read this advice on 'Mixing down'. Listen again to Part 2. Then note the points in this text which are additional to those given on the tape.

Mixing down

When mixing down, play back and listen to your master version through different speakers. If it still sounds good on cheap speakers, it passes the test. If possible, mix down on a later day to the recording. Have a break, as fresh ears hear things differently.

5 Similarly, do not mix on your own – someone else might point out things you have missed. And do not keep turning the volume up 'to hear things better'. Keep an eye on the volume and, if necessary, turn everything down and have a break. It will seem loud enough when you come back.

10 Above all, always keep in mind the overall sound. Do not listen to one instrument at the expense of others. Walk around the room while listening to a playback. Remember: sound is flexible and can be changed by the slightest factor, so use your ears.

Language study *Giving advice*

The interview and the text mention things to do and things not to do when making your own recordings. For example:

Things to do
   Leave it for a bit before you make the final copy.

Things not to do
   Make sure you don't go into the red or you'll get distortion.

Here are some other ways in which we can give advice in an informal way. Note how we can make the advice stronger.

Things to do
   1   *You **should** keep an eye on the recording level.*
   2   ***Always** keep an eye on the recording level.*
   3   *You **must always** keep an eye on the recording level.*

Things not to do
   1   *You **shouldn't** put the microphone too close to the drums.*
   2   ***Never** put the microphone too close to the drums.*
   3   *You **must never** put the microphone too close to the drums.*

Task 6

Write a list of things to do and things not to do when making a recording. Use information from the text and from the tape together with any information of your own. For example:

Things to do

   1   *You should listen to your master through different speakers.*

Things not to do

   2   *Don't keep turning the volume up to 'hear things better'.*

When you have finished, exchange lists with your partner. Do you agree with the list your partner has made? If not, discuss any disagreement with your partner.

8 Remote control

Tuning-in

Task 1

Which television and video recorder controls are operated by remote control buttons with these symbols?

1	⏻	4	◀◀	7	▶
2	🔇	5	▶▶	8	❚❚
3	☀	6	■	9	((●))

Task 2

Read paragraph 1 of this text. How many of the controls you identified in Task 1 are named in the text?

* *couch potatoes:* people who spend most of their time sitting on a couch (sofa) watching television

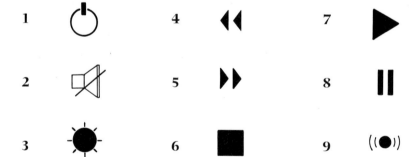

para

1

The widespread use of television remote control units has turned the British into a nation of couch potatoes*. Gone are all the fiddly knobs and buttons which once controlled picture contrast, colour brightness, volume, and so on. Nowadays we can change channel,
5 adjust the sound and picture, and call up a range of services on the teletext systems with the push of a button.

Reading *Information transfer*

A useful way of remembering the main points of what we read is to transfer the important information into a different form, such as a table or a diagram. In this unit, you are asked to transfer information from a text to a flowchart. Flowcharts are often used to describe processes.

Task 3

Now read paragraph 2 to complete the gaps in the flowchart, which shows how the remote control transmitter works.

para
2

The remote control unit contains keys and electronic components similar to those of a calculator. The keys are connected by a matrix of wires which cross beneath each individual key. Pressing a key
10   completes an electrical circuit, and a signal is sent to a microchip which, in turn, sends a series of on–off electrical pulses to a light-emitting diode (LED) at the front of the handset. A code spelt out by the length and spacing of these pulses switches on the LED. The LED flashes on and off to send an infra-red beam to the receiving
15   'eye' on the television set.

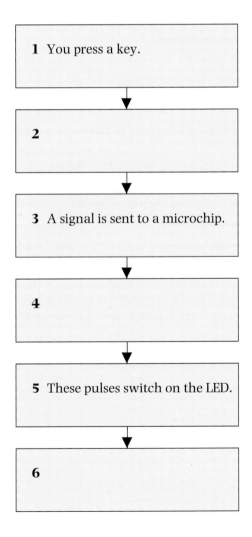

1 You press a key.

2

3 A signal is sent to a microchip.

4

5 These pulses switch on the LED.

6

Language study *Actions in sequence*

Study this flowchart, which describes what happens when the signals are received from the remote control.

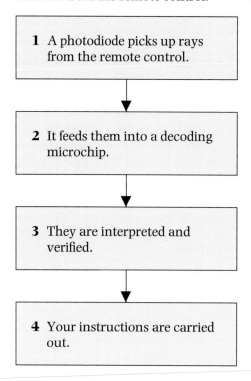

1 A photodiode picks up rays from the remote control.

2 It feeds them into a decoding microchip.

3 They are interpreted and verified.

4 Your instructions are carried out.

We can link two stages in the flowchart to show the sequence of events like this:

1 + 2   ***When*** *a photodiode picks up rays from the remote control, it feeds them into a decoding microchip.*

2 + 3   ***After*** *it feeds them into the microchip, they are interpreted and verified.*

3 + 4   ***Once*** *they are interpreted and verified, your instructions are carried out.*

The part of each sentence beginning with a time word – ***when, after, once*** – is called a time clause.

When shows that one stage is followed immediately by the next stage.
After simply shows the sequence of stages – 1 comes before 2.
Once emphasizes that one stage is complete before the next stage begins.

Task 4

Go back to the flowchart you made in Task 3. Write sentences to link stages 1 and 2, 3 and 4, and 5 and 6, using time clauses.

1 and 2 _____

_____

3 and 4 _____

_____

5 and 6 _____

_____

Speaking practice

Task 5

Work in pairs, **A** and **B**. Fill in the gaps in the block diagram and flowchart of a radar system with the help of your partner.

Ask questions like these:

> *What does the transmitter consist of?*
> *What does the oscillator do?*
> *Where is the signal generated?*
> *What generates the signal?*
> *What happens next/after that?*

Student A: Your diagram is on page 175.
Student B: Your diagram is on page 182.

Writing *Describing a system*

Task 6

You are going to write a brief description of the radar system, using the completed diagram to help you. Your description should answer these questions:

1 What does the radar system consist of?
2 What are the components of the transmitter?
3 What does the receiver consist of?
4 Where is the signal generated?
5 What happens to it after that?
6 If a target is hit, what happens to the reflected signal?
7 How does the receiver process the signal?
8 What happens to both signals finally?

The building blocks of texts are paragraphs. Each paragraph deals with a different question or set of related questions.

Divide these questions into three sets, then write one paragraph for each set of questions.

paragraph 1

_____

_____

_____

paragraph 2

_____

_____

paragraph 3

_____

_____

_____

Technical reading *Remote control system*

Task 7

Fill the gaps in this diagram with the help of the text which follows.

Stage	Function
audio oscillator	
	amplifies pulses to drive the LED
LED	

A remote control system

The block diagram of a simple remote control system is shown in Fig. 1. When the transmitter is switched on, infra-red signals are sent from the transmitter to the receiver. Pulsed signals are used to prevent interference from any constant infra-red background 'noise'.

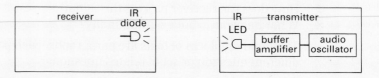

Fig. 1

5 To obtain these pulsed signals, electrical pulses are first generated at a frequency in the upper audio range by the audio oscillator in the transmitter. They are then amplified by the buffer amplifier to enable them to drive the light-emitting diode (LED). Finally, the electrical pulses are converted by the LED into pulsed infra-red radiation which
10 is directed at the receiver. Almost no visible light is emitted from the LED.

Task 8

Now fill in the gaps in this diagram with the help of the text which follows.

Components	Function
IC1	_____ and amplifier
R1, R2 and C2	
R3	
C1	

The circuit diagram of a remote control transmitter is shown in Fig. 2.

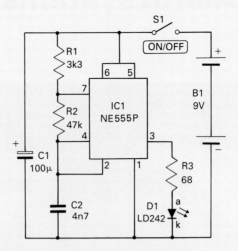

Fig. 2

In this circuit, both the oscillator and amplifier are combined in a
single chip integrated circuit (IC1). The frequency of the oscillator is
15   set by the external timing components R1, R2, and C2. The current
output of the amplifier is controlled by the resistor R3 which is
connected in series with the LED. Decoupling of the DC supply from
the pulsed output of the IC is provided by the electrolytic capacitor C1.

9 Alarm systems

Tuning-in

Task 1

Listen to this radio news item and complete the table below.

The Government's three-pronged attack on car crime aims to persuade:

	Group	Action
1	motor manufacturers	to fit _____
2	car owners	to be more vigilant about _____
3	insurance companies	to offer lower premiums for motorists who install _____

Task 2

Study the diagram at the top of the following page. Try to answer these questions:

1 What does this diagram show a circuit of?
2 How many detection devices does it show? Name them.
3 What warning device does it show?
4 Why is the control box switch operated with a key?
5 How does the system work?
6 What problem is there with this circuit?

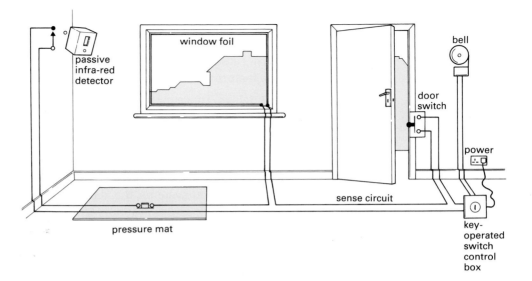

window foil

bell

passive infra-red detector

door switch

power

sense circuit

pressure mat

key-operated switch control box

Task 3

Work in groups of four. Find out how one of these devices works by reading the appropriate paragraph in this text. Your teacher will tell you which device to read about. Then explain briefly to your group how the device works.

1 door switch
2 window foil
3 pressure mat
4 passive infra-red detector

Detection devices

Magnetic switches

These are used on windows and doors. A magnet mounted on the moving part of the window or door trips a switch mounted on the frame when the window or door is opened.

Break detectors

These are fitted on the inside surface of glass in windows and doors.
5   Some use a thin metal foil which is glued around the edge of the glass: if the glass is broken the foil breaks too. Others are vibration sensors, and respond to the shock of the glass being broken.

Pressure mats

These are fitted under the carpet – at the bottom of the stairs, for example. The pressure of someone stepping on them causes two thin
10   metal plates inside to come in contact, setting off the alarm. Because they're constantly being walked on, pressure mats can get 'tired' quite quickly, and should be regularly tested and replaced if necessary.

Motion sensors

These may use passive infra-red, ultrasonic, or microwave energy to detect movement within their range.

Task 4

How could the system shown in Task 2 be improved? Note your ideas. Now read this text to check which of your ideas are described.

We can make the simple alarm circuit more effective by including some of these features.

Entry and exit delays These mean you won't set off the alarm when leaving or returning to the house. On the better systems, the delays
5 are adjustable. An audible warning during the delay period is a useful reminder.

Automatic cut-off This will stop the alarm after it has sounded for a set time, so that the noise doesn't go on for hours if you're not there to reset the system. In better systems, the alarm automatically resets at
10 the end of the alarm time.

Tamper protection The control panel incorporates sensors which will trigger the alarm if a burglar tries to force the box open.

Battery backup This means the alarm will continue to work in a power cut, or if an intruder disconnects the mains supply.

Task 5

Match each action with its consequence. Then identify the device or feature described. For example:

Action: *Someone moves within its range.*
Consequence: *It detects the movement.*
Device = *motion sensor*

Action		Consequence	
Action		**Consequence**	
1	A burglar disconnects the supply.	a	A magnet on the moving part trips a switch.
2	The glass is broken.	b	Tamper sensors trigger the alarm.
3	A door is opened.	c	The alarm continues to operate on batteries.
4	A window is opened.	d	Two thin metal plates come in contact.
5	You're not there to reset the system.	e	The foil breaks too.
6	A burglar tries to force the alarm open.	f	A magnet on the door trips a switch on the frame.
7	Someone steps on them.	g	The alarm stops after a set time.

Language study *If-sentences*

Study this action and its consequence:

Action: *A burglar tries to force the alarm open.*
Consequence: *Sensors trigger the alarm.*

We can link action and consequence like this:

1 ***If** a burglar tries to force the alarm open, sensors trigger the alarm.*
2 ***If** a burglar tries to force the alarm open, sensors will trigger the alarm.*
3 *Sensors will trigger the alarm **if** a burglar tries to force it open.*

Task 6   Complete these sentences with a suitable action or consequence.

1. If pressure mats are constantly walked on, ...
2. If you fit an exit delay, ...
3. If your system doesn't have an automatic cut-off, ...
4. If a burglar walks in front of a motion sensor, ...
5. Vibration sensors will respond if . . . .
6. Tamper sensors will trigger the alarm if . . . .
7. A magnet on the moving part trips a switch if . . . .
8. The alarm stops after a set time if . . . .

Speaking practice

Task 7   Work in pairs, **A** and **B**. Find out from your partner how to perform the tasks you have been set. Explain to your partner how to perform his/her tasks with the help of the diagrams provided.

Example:

a   **b**

Task: *Operating a mercury switch.*

Useful language:

> *How do you operate a mercury switch? You tilt it.*
> *How does a mercury switch work? By tilting it.*

Student A: Your tasks are on page 175.
Student B: Your tasks are on page 182.

Word study   *Word pairs, 1*

Task 8   Each word in column **A** often goes before one word from column **B**. For example, *integrated circuit* (**1f**). Find the other word pairs.

	A		B
1	integrated	a	sensor
2	circuit	b	cell
3	alternating	c	switch
4	primary	d	supply
5	zener	e	diode
6	remote	f	circuit
7	reed	g	current
8	surface	h	bias
9	vibration	i	control
10	reverse	j	diagram
11	mains	k	wave

Technical reading *Alarm systems*

Use information from the text below to complete the tables/answer the questions.

1 Complete this table.

Sensing device	Used to detect
LDR	
	heat
	sound

2 What effect does light have on an LDR?

3 What is the purpose of RV1 in Fig. 2 on page 53?

4 Use words from the text to complete the following table:

Term	Opposite
cut-off	saturation
fixed resistor	
increases	
energize	
slow	
to cause	
forward bias	

5 How is the transistor in Fig. 2 protected from a large back EMF?

The three stages of a simple alarm system are shown in Fig. 1.

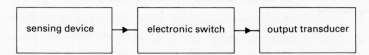

Fig. 1

The first stage is a sensing device that changes its resistance when it detects a particular form of energy. For example, a microphone may be used to detect sound, a thermistor to detect heat, or an LDR (light-
5 dependent resistor) to detect light.

The second stage is an electronic switch. In its simplest form, this could be a single transistor. The transistor switches between cut-off and saturation as the input resistance changes.

The third stage is an output transducer which is switched off and on by
10 the electronic switch. The output transducer could be a buzzer, a light, or a relay which operates a more powerful circuit.

An example of a simple alarm circuit is shown in Fig. 2.

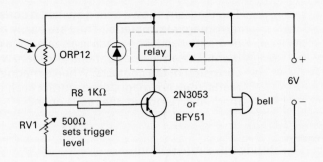

Fig. 2

The LDR forms a potential divider with the variable resistor RV1. When light falls on the LDR, its resistance decreases. This causes the base
15 voltage of the transistor and the bias current to increase. The transistor switches on and there is a rapid rise in the collector current until the transistor goes into saturation. The increased current causes the relay to operate and switch on the output circuit. The sensitivity of the input can be adjusted using RV1.

20 In a similar way, the relay is de-energized when the light source is removed from the LDR. A large back EMF, which would destroy the transistor, could be generated across the relay. To prevent this, a diode is connected in reverse bias across the relay.

Writing *Explanations*

Task 10

Explanations provide answers to *Why?* and *How?* questions. Try to answer these questions about the diagram below.

1 What does the diagram show?
2 Why are the reeds sealed in a glass envelope?
3 Why does the envelope contain nitrogen?
4 How does it operate?

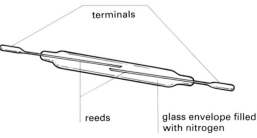

A reed switch

Now study this explanation, which has been written to answer the questions on the previous page.

> The diagram shows a reed switch. It consists of two reeds made of ferromagnetic material. They are easily magnetized and demagnetized. The reeds are sealed in a glass envelope to protect them. The envelope contains nitrogen, which helps to prevent
> 5 corrosion of the contacts. When a magnet is brought close to the reeds, they are magnetized, attract each other, and close. When the magnet is removed, the reeds open.

Task 11

Study this simple circuit.

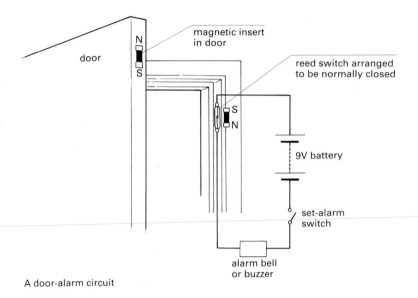

A door-alarm circuit

Explain what this diagram shows and how it operates. Your explanation should include answers to these questions:

1 What are the components?
2 How are they connected?
3 What is the state of the system when the door is closed?
4 What happens if the door is opened?
5 Why does this happen?

10 Radio

Tuning-in

Task 1 Study this diagram. Name five things, other than radio, which make use of electromagnetic waves.

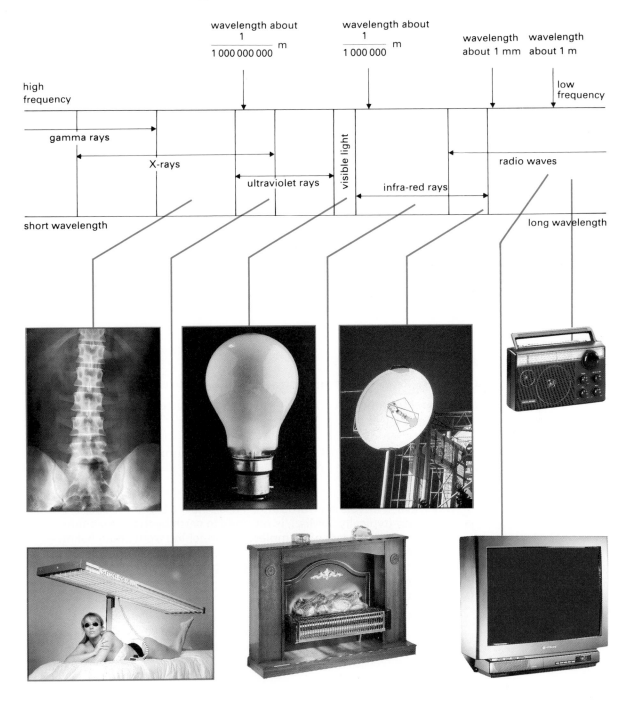

wavelength about $\dfrac{1}{1\,000\,000\,000}$ m

wavelength about $\dfrac{1}{1\,000\,000}$ m

wavelength about 1 mm

wavelength about 1 m

high frequency

low frequency

gamma rays

X-rays

ultraviolet rays

visible light

infra-red rays

radio waves

short wavelength

long wavelength

Reading *Information transfer*

In Unit 8, you transferred information from text to flowcharts. Here you will practise transferring information from text to tables and diagrams.

Task 2

Read this text and complete Table 1 below.

Propagation of radio waves

Radio waves from a transmitting aerial can travel in one or more of three different ways.

Surface or ground wave This travels along the ground, following the curvature of the earth's surface. Its range is limited mainly by the
5   extent to which energy is absorbed from it by the ground. Poor conductors, such as sand, absorb more strongly than water, and the higher the frequency the greater the absorption. The range is about 1500km at low frequencies (long waves).

Table 1

	Surface wave
Frequencies	
Travels	
Range	
Difficulties	

Task 3

Work in pairs, **A** and **B**.

Student A: Read the text on sky waves and complete your section of Table 2.

Student B: Read the text on space waves and complete your section of Table 2.

When you have finished, ask your partner for the information to complete the table.

Sky wave It travels skywards and, if it is below a certain critical
10   frequency (typically 30MHz), is returned to earth by the ionosphere. This consists of layers of air molecules stretching from about 80km above the earth to 500km. On striking the earth, the sky wave bounces back to the ionosphere where it is again gradually refracted and returned earthwards as if by 'reflection'. This continues until it is
15   completely attenuated.

The critical frequency varies with the time of day and the seasons. Sky waves of high frequencies can travel thousands of kilometres but at VHF and above they usually pass through the ionosphere into outer space.

20 **Space Wave** For VHF, UHF, and microwave signals, only the space wave, giving line of sight transmission, is effective. A range of up to 150km is possible on earth if the transmitting aerial is on high ground and there are no intervening obstacles such as hills, buildings, or trees. Space waves are also used for satellite communications.

Table 2

	Sky wave	Space wave
Frequencies		
Travels		
Range		
Difficulties		

Task 4

With the help of Tables 1 and 2, label the diagram using these labels:

a transmitting aerial   d space wave
b receiving aerial   e surface wave
c sky wave

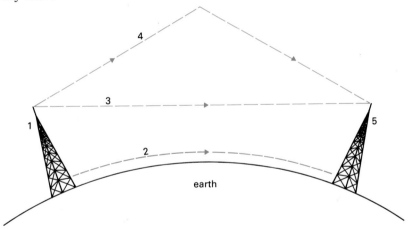

Language study   *Reduced time clauses*

Study these two actions:

1 *Ground waves pass over sand.*
2 *Ground waves lose energy.*

We can link these actions to make one sentence, using a time clause:

    When *ground waves pass over sand, they lose energy.*

Because the subject of both actions is the same – *ground waves* – there is a shorter method we can use to link the actions:

    When *pass**ing** over sand, ground waves lose energy.*

When + -ing shows that Action 2 happens during the same period as Action 1.

Now study these two actions:

1   *The sky wave strikes the earth.*
2   *The sky wave bounces back again.*

Again we can link these actions to make one sentence, using a time clause:

When *the sky wave strikes the earth, it bounces back again.*

We can also link the actions in a shorter way:

On stri**king** *the earth, the sky wave bounces back again.*

On + -ing shows that Action 2 follows immediately after Action 1.

Task 5

Link these pairs of actions. Use short ways when this is possible.

1 **a** The switch is closed.
   b Current flows through the primary of the transformer.

2 **a** The radar signal strikes a plane.
   b The radar signal is reflected.

3 **a** A cell discharges quickly.
   b A cell may become hot.

4 **a** The TV receives signals from the remote control.
   b The TV follows your instructions.

5 **a** The radar receiver receives the reflected signal.
   b The signal is compared with the transmitted signal.

6 **a** You choose a course in electronics.
   b You think carefully about your future.

7 **a** Microwave signals strike a high building.
   b Microwave signals are deflected.

8 **a** You make a recording.
   b You should ensure the recording levels are satisfactory.

9 **a** The alarm detects an intruder.
   b The alarm triggers an audible warning.

10 **a** The remote control button is pressed.
   b The television set changes channel.

Speaking practice

Task 6

Work in pairs, **A** and **B**. Fill the gaps in your table of frequency bands and their uses with the help of your partner. Ask questions like these:

What does VLF stand for / mean?
What are very low frequencies used for?
What is the frequency range of very low frequencies?

Frequency band	Some uses
Very low (VLF)	communication
3kHz–30kHz	with submarines

Student A: Your table is on page 176.
Student B: Your table is on page 183.

Word study   *Word formation*

Study the verb and two related nouns below. One noun is used for a component. The other is an abstract noun used for a property.

amplify   amplifier   amplification

Task 7

With the help of the reading passage, earlier units, and your own knowledge, fill the gaps in this table.

Verb	Noun (component)	Noun (property)
absorb	—	_____
attenuate	attenuator	_____
_____	—	communication
conduct	_____	conductivity
_____	inductor	_____
modulate	_____	modulation
reflect	reflector	_____
resist	_____	_____

Task 8

Listen to the words in the table. Try to mark the stressed syllable.

Technical reading   *Radio*

Task 9

Explain these abbreviations. Check your answers by looking quickly through the text below.

1 AF
2 RF
3 AM
4 FM

Radio frequency (RF) waves are used to carry audio frequency (AF) waves over long distances through the air. The audio signals can be combined with the RF carrier wave in such a way that it varies the amplitude of the carrier. This gives an amplitude-modulated (AM)
5 carrier wave (see Fig. 1).

AF signal   RF carrier   modulated RF carrier

Fig. 1

In a frequency-modulated (FM) wave, the audio signal is combined with the RF carrier wave to vary the frequency of the carrier (see Fig. 2).

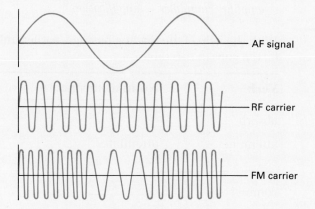

Fig. 2

The block diagram of a radio is shown in Fig. 3 below. The tuner
10 selects the required RF wave from those picked up by the aerial. The selected RF wave is amplified and passed to the detector, which separates the audio modulation from the RF carrier wave. The audio frequency amplifier then amplifies the audio signal to make it strong enough to drive the loudspeaker.

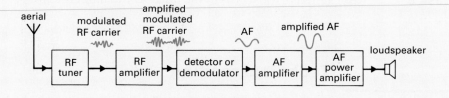

Fig. 3

Tuner

15 A typical radio tuner circuit consists of an inductor and capacitor connected in parallel (see Fig. 4). The size of the aerial inductance coil can be kept small by winding it on a ferrite rod core.

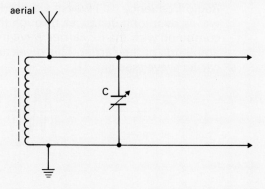

Fig. 4

The RF waves fed to the tuner cause the circuit to oscillate. The impedance of the circuit is smallest and the oscillation is greatest at a
20 particular frequency known as the resonant frequency. This frequency is determined by the values of the inductance and the capacitance. By using a variable capacitor, the circuit can be tuned to the required radio frequency, and the selected RF wave passed on to the RF amplifier.

Task 10

Identify the waves. Use these terms:

1 FM carrier   **2** AM carrier   **3** AF signal   **4** RF carrier

a 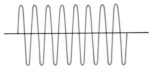   **c**

b 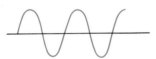   **d**

Task 11

Explain what happens at each stage in this flowchart, which shows how a radio works. The first and last stage are done for you.

Component		**Function**
1	aerial	receives weak RF signals
2	RF tuner	
3	RF amplifier	
4	detector	
5	AF amplifier	
6	loudspeaker	converts the audio signal into sound

61

Writing *Describing a process*

When describing a process, it can be useful first to make a flowchart like the one in Task 11, showing the stages in the correct sequence. You can then expand the flowchart to include a brief description of what happens at each stage.

The next step is to turn your flowchart into a written description. You can help your readers by marking the order of the stages with sequence markers. The most common markers are:

Firstly,   Next,   Following that,
Then,   After that,   Finally,

We can summarize this advice with a flowchart:

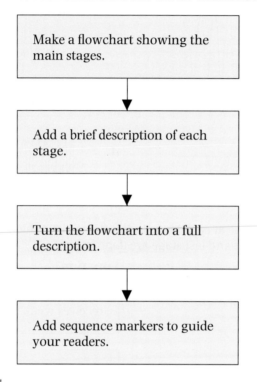

Make a flowchart showing the main stages.

Add a brief description of each stage.

Turn the flowchart into a full description.

Add sequence markers to guide your readers.

Task 12

Describe how a radio deals with a radio signal. Base your description on the flowchart in Task 11.

11 Transistor characteristics

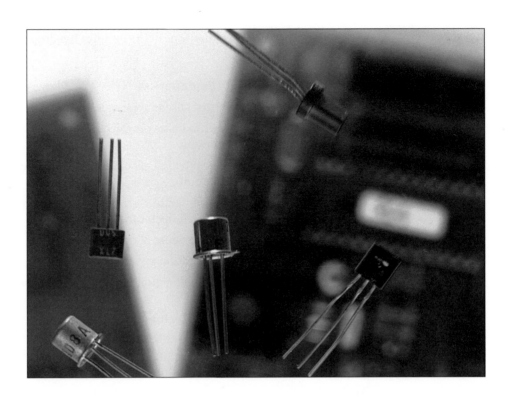

Tuning-in

Task 1

Study this table from a suppliers' catalogue of transistor characteristics. What do these abbreviations mean? Compare your answers with your partner.

1 V **2** mA **3** mW **4** MHz **5** AF

Table 1

Small-signal low-frequency silicon transistors

Type no.	Price each	Case style	Material	V_{CEO} (max) V	V_{CBO} (max) V	V_{EBO} (max) V	I_c(max) mA	P_{TOT} (max) mW	Typ h_{FE} @I_c	Typ f_T (MHz)	Application
BC107B	20p	T018	NPN	45	50	6	100	300	290@2mA	300	AF driver (comp to BC177)
BC108C	20p	T018	NPN	20	30	5	100	300	520@2mA	300	General purpose (comp to BC178)
BC109C	20p	T018	NPN	20	30	5	100	300	520@2mA	300	Low noise, high gain amp (comp to BC179)
BC168C	14p	T092	NPN	20	30	5	100	300	650@2mA	85	General purpose
BC169C	14p	T092	NPN	20	30	5	50	300	650@2mA	150	High gain, low noise amp
BC183L	10p	T092	NPN	30	45	5	200	300	>125@2mA	150	General purpose (comp to BC213L)
BC184L	12p	T092	NPN	30	45	5	200	300	>125@2mA	150	Low noise, high gain amp (comp to BC214L)
BC212L	10p	T092	PNP	−50	−60	−5	200	300	>60@2mA	200	AF driver (comp to BC182L)
BC213L	10p	T092	PNP	−30	−45	−5	200	300	>80@2mA	200	General purpose (comp to BC183L)
BC214L	12p	T092	PNP	−30	−45	−5	200	300	>140@2mA	200	Low noise, high gain amp (comp to BC184L)

Reading *Locating and applying information*

Locating information about components quickly from a table and using that information to solve a practical problem are useful skills for technicians and engineers. In the task which follows, note the time you take to answer the questions. Compare times within your class.

Task 2

Use Table 1 and these explanations of the column headings to answer the questions which follow.

Heading	**Explanation**
Case style	transistor case and pin connections
V_{CEO} (max)	maximum value of collector-emitter voltage with base left open-circuit
V_{CBO} (max)	maximum value of collector-base voltage with emitter left open-circuit
V_{EBO} (max)	maximum value of (reverse) emitter-base voltage with collector left open-circuit
I_C (max)	maximum value of collector current
P_{TOT} (max)	maximum total power dissipation
Typ h_{FE}	typical small-signal current gain (in common-emitter configuration)
@ I_C	value of collector current at which the small-signal current gain is quoted
Typ f_T	transition frequency (i.e. the frequency at which the common-emitter current gain falls to 1)
Application	recommended use for the device

1 What's the recommended use for a BC214L?
2 What's the maximum collector current for a BC169C?
3 Which transistor can be used in a complementary configuration with a BC183L?
4 Could you use a BC109C in a circuit where the collector-emitter voltage will be in the range 10–30 volts?
5 What is the common-emitter current gain for a BC168C at a frequency of 85Mhz?

Task 3

Working with your partner, try these more difficult questions. You have the following transistors available: BC168C, BC169C, BC212L, BC214L. Which of them is most suitable for use in a circuit:

1 with a collector current greater than 100mA and a collector-emitter voltage between −10V and −35V?
2 with a common-emitter current gain greater than 100 and a collector current greater than 100mA?
3 which requires a common-emitter current gain greater than 200 at a frequency of 100MHz?
4 which is a low noise preamp with a collector current greater than 80mA?
5 with a collector current of 70mA and a common-emitter current gain greater than 600?

Writing 1 *Describing transistor characteristics*

Task 4

Complete this description of a BC108C using the information in Table 1 on page 63 and the explanations in Task 2.

The BC108C is an NPN transistor with a [1]_____ style case. It can pass a maximum collector current of [2]_____ mA.

With the base left open, the collector-emitter junction would break down at [3]_____ V. The collector-base breakdown [4]_____ , with the emitter disconnected, is 30V. The [5]_____ junction breakdown voltage is 5V when the collector is left open. These are the highest usable voltages for this transistor.

The transistor dissipates a [6]_____ power of 300mW. When connected in common-emitter configuration, the small-signal current gain is 520 measured at a collector current of [7]_____ mA. Typically, this gain would be reduced to 1 at a frequency of [8]_____ MHz. The transistor is a [9]_____ device which can be used in complementary configuration with a [10]_____

Task 5

Now write your own description of a BC214L, based on the text you have just completed in Task 4.

_____

_____

_____

_____

_____

_____

_____

_____

_____

_____

_____

_____

_____

_____

_____

_____

_____

_____

_____

Writing 2 *Ordering components*

Task 6

Study this letter.

Satex S.p.A.
Via di Pietra Papa
00146 Roma

Currie Electronics
P.O. Box 3
Patten
Essex
SS2 3MQ
UK

17 April 19_ _

Dear Sir

Please could you supply the following components:

Description	Quantity	Price each	Total £/p
BD140 transistors	8	26p	£2.08
dielectric trimmer SW trim 10 pF	1	£6.45	£6.45
		Handling charge	£1.00
		TOTAL	£9.53

I enclose a bank draft(no.1563526)for nine pounds
and fifty-three pence.

Yours faithfully

Rino Rumiati

Now write your own letter ordering transistors, using the information given in
Table 1 on page 63.

12 Metal detector

Tuning-in

Task 1
Study this newspaper headline. What do you think the story will be about?

£½ M TREASURE FOUND BURIED IN SCOTTISH FIELD

Task 2
Now listen to a radio news item which refers to the same story and answer these questions:

1 How did Mr Swanston find the coins?
2 How does he know when his detector has found something made of metal?
3 Why did he ask his friends to help?
4 How many coins did they find?
5 How old are the coins?
6 What will happen to the coins?
7 Who will benefit from this?

Task 3
Read the short text below, then discuss these questions:

1 How can you create a changing magnetic field?
2 How can you detect a voltage created in a buried object?

> **Metal detectors,** despite their technical complexity, are based on a few very simple principles. The most important is that of electromagnetic induction. This means that if an object is placed in a changing magnetic field, an electrical voltage is created in the object.

...

Task 4   Check your answers to Task 3 with the help of the text and diagrams.

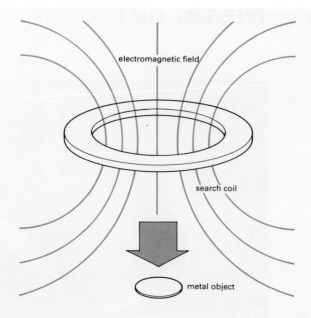

Alternating current (AC) is applied to the coil in the search head from the battery in the control box. This creates an ever-changing electromagnetic field around the coil. An electric current is induced in any metal object the coil passes near.

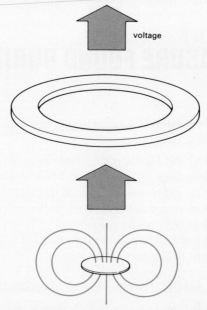

5   The current induced in the metal object produces its own magnetic field, which in turn induces a voltage in the search coil, as the alternating current changes direction.

The circuitry in the control box senses this reaction and converts the voltage into an audible note, which is sent to the headset. As the metal
10   object is approached, the sound in the headset becomes louder, or changes pitch.

Task 5   Label each step in this flowchart with the correct letter from the list below. The
first one is done for you.

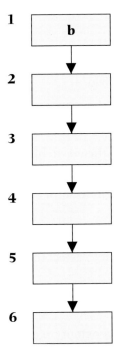

a   Magnetic field around the object
b   AC voltage in the search coil
c   Electric current in the metal object
d   Induced voltage in the search coil
e   Note heard in headset
f   Magnetic field around the coil

Reading   *Linking what you read with what you know*

Not everything in a text is clearly stated. When reading, we have to make links
between what we read and what we already know about the subject.

Read this brief text and try to answer this question:

Can metal detectors be used to trace water pipes under a street?

> Metal detectors can find buried metal. They were developed for military
> purposes to locate hidden explosives. They operate on the principle of
> electromagnetic induction.

To answer the question, you have to link knowledge from the text and
knowledge of your own.

From the text we know:
   Metal detectors can find buried metal.

From your own knowledge you know:
   Most water pipes are metal. They are buried under streets.

The more knowledge we have about our subject and about the world in
general, the easier it is to learn new things when we read.

Read the text below, then look at these statements. Are they true or false? You may need to use your own knowledge as well as information from the text.

1   Any metal detector can discriminate between gold and other metals.

2   Gold necklaces are found quite often.

3   The search coil is connected directly to a battery.

4   Metal detectors require a changing magnetic field.

5   The metal detector can only locate metals which contain iron or are magnetic.

6   Metal detectors are only used by treasure hunters.

7   Passing a current through the search coil and then switching it off, creates a pulse of magnetism round the coil.

8   All metal detectors are fitted with a flashing light to show when an object has been found.

9   Large objects are easier to find than small objects.

10 A coin horizontal to the surface is more difficult to detect than one vertical to the surface.

A metal detector is essential for today's amateur treasure hunter. But only the most expensive detector can reveal the difference between worthless items, such as pull-ring tops from soft drink cans or silver foil, and a rare find such as the gold necklace discovered by one
5   enthusiast last year.

Electronic metal detectors use the principle of electromagnetic induction. This means that, if an object is placed in a changing magnetic field, an electrical voltage is created in the object. In a metal detector, an electrical current is passed through a coil of wire, called
10 the search coil, to create a magnetic field. An alternating current (AC) generator converts the direct current (DC) from the battery into the AC needed to drive the coil. As AC regularly reverses direction, it produces the necessary ever-changing magnetic field.

Currents are created in a metal object which comes within this
15 magnetic field by a process known as induction. This is because all metals conduct electricity. When a current is induced in a metal object (for example, a buried coin), this in turn produces its own magnetic fields. These magnetic fields are capable of inducing a small amount of electricity in the detector's search coil itself.

20 The simplest kind of metal detector is the pulse induction type. A powerful current is passed from the battery through the search coil and then switched off. The pulse of magnetism causes current to flow in any target objects below the ground. But unlike the current in the search coil, the current in the object cannot be switched off; it has to
25 die away naturally. As it dies, the current in the object reactivates the search coil. This voltage is then amplified to indicate with a sound or a flashing light that an object has been found.

The effectiveness of a metal detector depends on the size and position of the object and how far beneath the gound it is buried. For example,
30 a coin buried edge-on to the search coil is much harder to detect than the same coin buried face up.

Language study *Grammar links*

Sentences in a text are held together by grammar links. Note the links in this paragraph:

Metal detectors are used to locate hidden metal objects such as water pipes. They contain a search coil and a control box. The coil is mounted in the search head. When an AC voltage from the box is applied to the coil, a magnetic field is created around it. In turn this induces a current in any metal object the head passes over.

This text illustrates some common grammar links:

Nouns become pronouns:
   metal detectors becomes *they.*

Repeated nouns change from *a* to *the* and sometimes words are dropped:
   a search coil becomes *the coil.*

Clauses and even sentences become *this* or *that*:
   a magnetic field is created around it becomes *this.*

Task 7

Now mark the grammar links in this paragraph by joining the words in italics with the words they refer to:

When an AC voltage is applied to the search coil, a magnetic field is produced around *it*. If there is a metal object under the ground, *the field* induces an electric current in *the object*. *The induced current* in turn creates a magnetic field around the object. *This* induces a voltage in the search coil. *The induced voltage* is converted into an audible note by the circuitry in the control box. *This sound* guides the treasure hunter to *the buried object*.

Word study *Transitive verbs*

Note these verbs, which are used often in electronics:

   generate   induce   detect

They are transitive verbs. This means they are followed by a direct object and can be used in the passive (when the object becomes the subject).

Active verb:
   The magnetic field **induces** *a voltage.*

Passive verb:
   A voltage **is induced** *by the magnetic field.*

In electronics these verbs take a limited range of objects. Study the following examples from this book:

   induce + a voltage/a noise/hum/a current

   generate + electrical pulses/a large EMF/signals

   detect + a movement/a voltage/a form of energy/sound/heat

Task 8

Complete each sentence with *generate*, *induce* or *detect*. Each sentence is from a text in this book.

1 The magnetic field ――――――― an electric current in the metal object.

2 A microphone may be used to ――――――― sound.

3 The oscillator ――――――― pulses at a fixed frequency of 32 768 Hz.

4 The magnetic field ――――――― a voltage in the search coil.

5 Noise is also ――――――― by the low-frequency mains supply.

6 Motion sensors may use microwave energy to ――――――― movement within their range.

7 Electrical pulses are first ――――――― at a frequency in the upper audio range by the audio oscillator.

8 The first stage is a sensing device that changes its resistance when it ――――――― a particular form of energy.

Task 9

Convert means to change something from one form to another. Study the following example from this book.

> An AC generator converts the DC from the battery into the AC needed to drive the coil.

Identify the components from these descriptions:

1 It converts AF signals into sound waves.
2 It converts electronic pulses into infra-red pulses.
3 It converts digital signals into analogue signals.
4 It converts an electrical signal into a visual signal.

Describe the action of the following, using *convert*:

5 a rectifier
6 a microphone
7 an analogue-to-digital converter
8 an audio amplifier

Writing   *Linking facts and ideas, 2*

Task 10

Link each pair of statements using the word or phrase provided. Omit unnecessary words and make any other changes required.

1 *for*
A metal detector is a device.
A metal detector locates hidden metal objects.

2 *to ... but*
The metal detector was developed for military purposes.
The metal detector was developed to find buried explosives.
Nowadays the metal detector is also used to locate pipes, cables and lost valuables.

3 *to*
Special detectors are used at airports.
Detectors are used to screen passengers for concealed weapons.

4 *which*
All detectors work on the same principle.
The principle is electromagnetic induction.

5 *if*
An object is placed in a changing magnetic field.
An electrical voltage is created in the object.

6 *when*
An AC voltage is applied to the search coil.
An ever-changing electromagnetic field is created around the search coil.

7 *if*
The coil passes near a metal object.
An electric current is induced in the metal object.

8 *which*
The electric current produces a magnetic field around the object.
The magnetic field induces a voltage in the search coil.

9 *when*
The circuitry senses this reaction.
The circuitry changes the voltage into an audible note.

10 *as*
The coil approaches the object.
The audible note becomes louder and louder.

Task 11

Form your completed statements into an explanation of how metal detectors work. Your explanation should consist of two paragraphs.

13 Music centre

Tuning-in

Task 1

Study this picture of a music centre.

1 What forms of audio input does it have?
2 What other forms of audio input might be added?

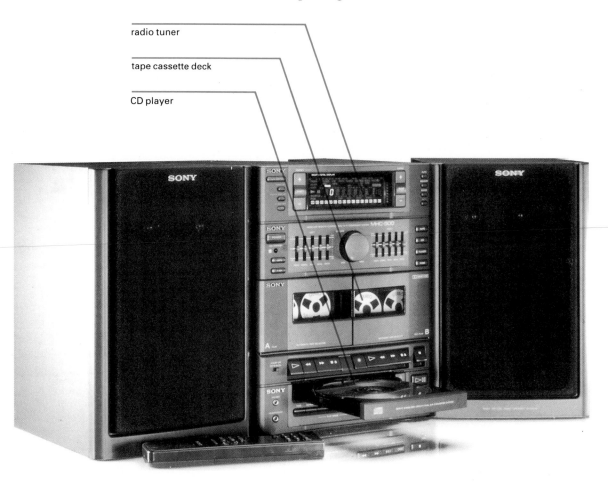

radio tuner

tape cassette deck

CD player

Fig. 1

Task 2

Read this text to check your answer to question 1 of Task 1.

Fig. 1 shows a music centre. It contains a number of audio input devices: a CD player, a radio tuner, and a tape cassette deck. These allow the user to play music recorded in different formats. All these devices share a common amplifier and speaker system. Each part of
5 the music centre is stacked one on top of the other.

Task 3

Read the rest of the text to find out:

1 the function of a pre-amplifier
2 the function of a power amplifier
3 the function of a graphic equalizer
4 the difference between a hi-fi and a midi-fi system

As Fig. 2 shows, the common amplifier is made up of two sections. The first section is the pre-amplifier (pre-amp), which provides tone, volume, and balance controls as well as amplification of the input signal voltages. The second section is the power amplifier (power
10 amp). This amplifies the power of the pre-amp signals to enable them to drive the loudspeaker system.

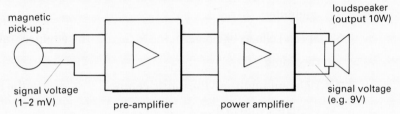

Fig. 2

Some music centres also contain a graphic equalizer. This allows the user to adjust the amplification of particular frequency ranges by moving an array of slider controls. In this way the reproduced sound
15 can be varied to suit different acoustic conditions.

A music centre can be classified as a hi-fi (high-fidelity) system or a mid-fi system depending on the quality of its sound reproduction.

Language study *Allowing and preventing verbs*

What happens as a result of . . .

closing the switch?
opening the switch?

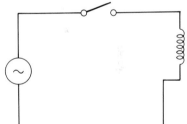

Closing the switch:
We can describe the result using these verbs:

| *Closing the switch* | ***allows*** ***permits*** ***enables*** | *current **to** flow through the coil.* |

Note that verbs like *allow* are followed by *to* and the infinitive.

Opening the switch:
We can describe the result using these verbs:

| *Opening the switch* | ***prevents*** ***stops*** | *current **from** flow**ing** through the coil.* |

Note that verbs like *prevent* are followed by *from* and the *-ing* form.

Task 4

Now fill in the gap in each sentence with an allowing or preventing verb. Also put each verb in brackets in the correct form.

1. A graphic equalizer _____ the user (adjust) the amplification of different frequency ranges.

2. A fuse _____ a sudden rise in current (damage) equipment.

3. A mixing desk _____ the sound engineer (improve) the quality of the sound recorded.

4. A heatsink _____ output transistors (overheat).

5. A surge suppressor _____ large current fluctuations (damage) computers.

6. Special effects like reverb _____ the engineer (alter) the sound of the recording.

7. Different inputs on the music centre _____ the user (play) CDs, cassettes, and MDs.

8. A safety tab _____ the user (erase) the tape by accident.

Task 5

Study this circuit of a burglar alarm. It contains a relay. The relay is shown in its unenergized form.

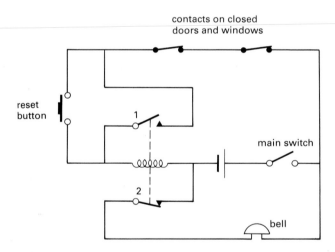

Now fill in the gaps in this description with appropriate verbs like *allow* or *prevent*, and put each verb in brackets in the correct form. Compare your answers with your partner.

Closing the main switch [1]_____ current (pass) from the battery through the bell. As a result the bell rings. Pressing the reset button [2]_____ current (flow) through the relay coil. This energizes the coil so that switch 1 closes and switch 2 opens. Opening switch 2 [3]_____ current (flow) through the bell.

When any contact on a door or window is opened, this [4]_____ current (pass) through the relay coil. As a result switch 1 opens and switch 2 closes. This [5]_____ current (flow) from the battery to the bell, and the alarm rings.

Speaking practice

Task 6

Work in pairs, **A** and **B**.

When choosing an amplifier for a particular system, it is important to know about the following characteristics:

voltage gain	input impedance
frequency response	output impedance
distortion	supply voltage
S/N ratio	

By the end of this task, you should be able to understand general amplifier specifications.

Student A: Your task and text are on pages 176–177.
Student B: Your task and text are on pages 183–184.

Writing   *Adding information to a text*

Study this brief text about noise.

> Noise can be a problem with amplifiers. There are several types of noise. One is crackle and another is hum.

Study this additional information:

Noise is any unwanted signals.
Crackle is produced randomly inside circuit components.
Hum is induced by the mains supply.

We can add the additional information like this:

*Noise, **which is any unwanted signals**, can be a problem with amplifiers. There are several types of noise. One is crackle, **which is produced randomly inside circuit components**, and another is hum, **which is induced by the mains supply**.*

When the information is additional, it is put in commas. For example:

*Noise, **which is any unwanted signals**, can be a problem with amplifiers.*

Without the words in bold, the sentence makes good sense.

Noise can be a problem with amplifiers.

When the information is essential to the meaning of the statement, commas are not used. For example:

*Noise **which is produced inside components** is called crackle.*

Without the words in bold, the sentence would not make sense.

Look at the diagram below and read the text opposite. Add information from the diagram to the text. The information added should answer the questions in brackets within the text. The first paragraph is done for you as an example.

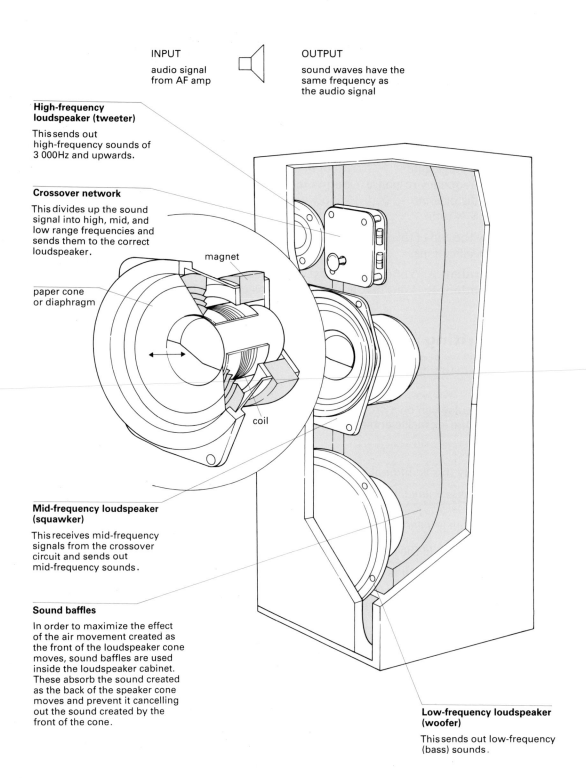

INPUT
audio signal
from AF amp

OUTPUT
sound waves have the
same frequency as
the audio signal

**High-frequency
loudspeaker (tweeter)**

This sends out
high-frequency sounds of
3 000Hz and upwards.

Crossover network

This divides up the sound
signal into high, mid, and
low range frequencies and
sends them to the correct
loudspeaker.

magnet

paper cone
or diaphragm

coil

**Mid-frequency loudspeaker
(squawker)**

This receives mid-frequency
signals from the crossover
circuit and sends out
mid-frequency sounds.

Sound baffles

In order to maximize the effect
of the air movement created as
the front of the loudspeaker cone
moves, sound baffles are used
inside the loudspeaker cabinet.
These absorb the sound created
as the back of the speaker cone
moves and prevent it cancelling
out the sound created by the
front of the cone.

**Low-frequency loudspeaker
(woofer)**

This sends out low-frequency
(bass) sounds.

Loudspeakers

The loudspeaker is the last important component of a music centre. It converts signals from the AF amplifier into sound waves (*What is the frequency of the sound waves?*).

Example

*The loudspeaker is the last important component of a music centre. It converts signals from the AF amplifier into sound waves **which have the same frequency as the AF signals.***

A loudspeaker consists of a cone (*What is the cone made of?*), a coil, and a fixed magnet. The coil (*What is the coil attached to?*) is free to vibrate within the magnet. As AC signals from the amplifier pass through the coil, they create an alternating magnetic field. The interaction of this field with the fixed field of the magnet causes the coil to vibrate. The cone also vibrates and produces sound waves. The bigger the signal from the amplifier, the larger the vibration of the cone and hence the louder the sound.

Speakers for hi-fi systems usually contain up to three individual units: a tweeter (*What kind of sounds does it send out?*), a squawker (*What kind of sounds does it send out?*), and a woofer (*What kind of sounds does it send out?*). These are served by a crossover network (*What does it do?*). They also contain sound baffles (*What do they do?*).

Technical reading *Stereo power amplifiers*

Task 8

Try to answer these questions about amplifiers, then read the text to see if you are correct.

1 What is meant by 'complementary transistors'?
2 What prevents power transistors from overheating?
3 What is stereo sound?
4 What is the purpose of a balance control?

Power amplification is required to drive low impedance loudspeakers. Many power amplifiers use a pair of complementary transistors, i.e. one transistor is a PNP type and the other is an NPN type. The characteristics of these transistors must be carefully matched. This
5 matched pair is connected in a push–pull configuration as shown in Fig. 1.

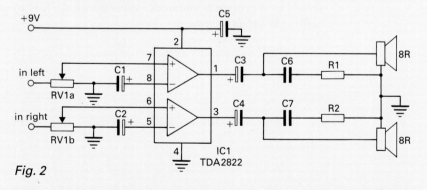

Fig. 1

This arrangement causes TR1 to be turned on and TR2 to be turned off during the positive half-cycle of the input signal. During the negative half-cycle, TR2 is turned on and TR1 is turned off. This means that the
10 input signal is alternately 'pushed' and 'pulled' through the loudspeaker. Because power transistors dissipate a lot of heat, they must be attached to large heatsinks.

For stereo sound, two identical amplifiers are used (see Fig. 2).

Fig. 2

One channel amplifies the signals for the left-hand speaker and the
15 other channel amplifies the signals for the right-hand speaker. In this case, a balance control is required to adjust the relative amplification of each channel.

14 Day release student

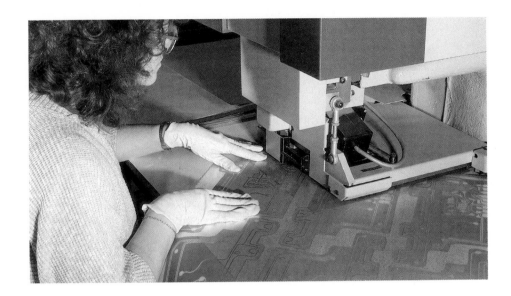

Listening

Shirley Sutton is a day release student. She talks here about her studies, her work, and her ambitions. The interview is in four parts. You are going to listen first for Shirley's opinions, then for details.

Task 1

Before you listen to Part 1, find out what *day release* means. With a partner try to list the advantages and disadvantages of such a form of study.

Now listen to Part 1 of the interview. Note any advantages and disadvantages of day release which Shirley mentions.

Advantages

_____

_____

Disadvantages

_____

_____

Task 2

Do you think electronics is a good career for women? Give reasons for your answer.

Now listen to Part 2 to find what Shirley's views are.

Shirley's views

_____

_____

Task 3

Find out what an *assembly line* is. Would you like to work on one? Give reasons for your answer.

⌨ Now listen to Part 3 to find out what Shirley's views are.

Shirley's views

_____

_____

_____

Task 4

What are your ambitions? What would you like to do at the end of your course?

⌨ Listen to Part 4 and find out what Shirley's ambitions are.

Shirley's ambitions

_____

_____

Task 5 ⌨ Listen to the tape again. This time listen for detail. Try to answer these questions:

Part 1

1   Name of course   _____

2   Length (years)   _____

3   Study (days per week)   _____

Part 2

4   Class size   _____

5   Number of males   _____

6   Number of females   _____

Part 3

7   What does her company make?
8   How long has she worked there?
9   What did she assemble?
10 What did she need before she could get promotion?

Part 4

11 What will she become at the end of the course?
12 How much extra experience does she need to become a test engineer?
13 What other route is there for promotion to test engineer?
14 Why does she reject the idea of full-time study for her HNC?

Language study   *Would*

Study this extract from the interview. The interviewer asks Shirley what she wants to do after the course.

Shirley: *Well, I hope to become a test engineer.*
Interviewer: *A test engineer. What **would** that involve?*

Why doesn't he ask, 'What will that involve?'?

Later he asks Shirley about her possible plans to take a Higher National Certificate course.

Shirley: *I **would** like to think that I **would** go on and do an HNC.*
Interviewer: ***Would** that be full-time?*
Shirley: *No, day release. If I were to leave my job, I **wouldn't** get it back.*

Why doesn't he ask, 'Will that be full-time?'?
Why doesn't she answer, 'If I leave my job, I won't get it back.'?

Would is used to show that the events described are not real at this time. They may happen in the future, but at present they are only possibilities. *Would* implies a hidden *if*. For example:

What would that involve? (***if you became a test engineer***)
Would that be full-time? (***if you took the HNC course***)

Task 6

Here is part of an interview with another student, Philip. Fill in the blanks with *will* or *would* or the reduced forms *'ll* and *'d* where appropriate.

I What ^{1}_____ you do when you leave college?

P I hope to work in local television.

I What kind of work ^{2}_____ you like to do?

P I ^{3}_____ like to be a sound technician. That ^{4}_____ give me a chance to work with a camera team on location.

I Is there any other kind of work you ^{5}_____ enjoy?

P Maybe working for a recording studio. But it all depends on my exams.

I When ^{6}_____ you take your finals?

P In June.

I And how soon after that ^{7}_____ you start applying for jobs?

P I've already started.

Word study *Word pairs, 2*

Task 7

Find one word which can pair with each of the following words. For example:
alternating/direct + *current*

1 carrier/ground/surface/sky/space + _____

2 zener/tunnel/light-emitting + _____

3 primary/secondary/NiCad + _____

4 audio/power/radio-frequency + _____

5 balance/tone/remote/volume + _____

6 mercury/double-pole/reed + _____

7 tuned/integrated/printed + _____

8 block/circuit + _____

15 Drum machine

Tuning-in

Task 1

Discuss these questions:

1 What do you think a drum machine does?
2 What do you think these keys refer to on a drum machine?

  kick   snare   closed hat   open hat

Task 2

Match each text on the following page to the correct step in the process of sampling and reproducing the sound of a drum digitally.

1

3

4

2

5

a When the drum pad is pressed, the stored information is decoded and produces an electronic signal.

b The signal is sliced into many 'samples', each one a snapshot of the strength of the signal at one particular moment. This information is converted into binary code and then stored in the machine's memory.

c When the drum is hit, it produces sound waves.

d The signal is turned into sound waves through an amplifier, and the drum sound is heard.

e The sound waves reach the microphone and are converted into an electrical signal.

Reading 1 *Recognizing topic*

A useful reading skill is skimming, which is to be able to recognize quickly which part of a text deals with a particular topic. Paragraphs usually deal with one topic or sub-topic.

Task 3

Read through the text quickly to find which paragraphs describe:

a analogue recording
b what *quantize* means
c the advantage of digital sound
d what happens when one of the drum buttons is pressed
e how sound samples are stored in a drum machine
f in brief what the machine does

Drum machine   *para*

A drum machine stores sound which has been recorded digitally.   1
The machine's read-only memory (ROM) stores sounds which have
been pre-recorded from the original instruments. By pressing the
pads which correspond to particular sounds, you can create your
5 own songs and rhythms without ever touching a drum kit. Each
sound can be played at any speed and in thousands of different
combinations.

When we hear sound, our ears are detecting changes in air   2
pressure. These changes in pressure, which might be caused by
10 vibrating a guitar string or banging a drum, are sound waves. To
record these, the wave patterns in the air are converted by a
microphone into electrical signals. The voltage and frequency of
these signals correspond exactly to the fluctuations in pressure of
the original wave. This is called analogue recording.

15 Instead of recording the sound waves continuously, a drum **3**
   machine is programmed with sounds that have been 'sampled'
   from the electrical signals produced by the microphone. This
   means that measurements are taken at frequent regular intervals
   and then recorded as binary code.

20 The advantage of digital sound is that it has only two electrical **4**
   conditions: on and off. Sounds recorded in this way remain
   accurate.

When you press one of the drum pads, a signal is sent to the **5**
microprocessor inside the machine which tells it which button is
25 being pressed. How hard you press and for how long, tells the
microprocessor how loud and at which tempo the sound should be.
The sounds are then stored in the memory blocks. This means that
you can repeat a pattern of drum sounds as many times as you like.

The digital-to-analogue converter changes the binary signals back **6**
30 into electrical impulses so that they can be played back through an
amplifier. The machine can also quantize, or shift the sounds being
played, so that each is rhythmically perfect. If you hit a note a little
ahead or behind the beat, the machine will automatically place the
drum hit right on the beat.

Reading 2 *Recognizing similar meaning*

In English the same idea can be expressed in many different ways.

Choose the statement, **a**, **b**, or **c**, which is closest in meaning to this statement
from the text:

> *When we hear sound, our ears are detecting changes in air pressure.*

a Changes in the pressure of the air around us are what we hear as sound.
b Hearing is really only changes in air pressure.
c Our hearing depends on the pressure of the air around us.

Task 4

Find sentences in the text above which are similar in meaning to the following
statements. Compare your answers with your partner. Try to reach agreement
on the right answer.

1 You don't need to play drums to make drum music; you need only touch the
switches which match the sounds you want.
2 The memory of a drum machine contains pre-recorded sounds from drum kits.
3 A microphone records sound by converting changes in air pressure to electrical
signals.
4 The patterns of the sound waves are matched by the characteristics of the
electrical signals.
5 Signals are sampled regularly and often, and stored in binary form.
6 Digital sound stays true to the original.
7 Pressing one of the buttons indicates to the processor the loudness and speed of
the music to be played.
8 You cannot make a mistake with the beat because the drum machine corrects
any errors by itself.

Language study   *-ing forms*

Words which end in *-ing* and sometimes behave like nouns are called '*-ing* forms'. They often refer to actions, processes and activities. Examples from the text on pages 85–86 are:

pressing   touching   vibrating   banging   recording

They are often used when there are no ordinary nouns available. For example:

*This receiver has very sensitive **tuning**.*

They are used after prepositions. For example:

***Without touching** a drum, you can make any drum sound you like.*

Task 5   Use the correct form of the word in brackets in each of these sentences:

1   With a drum machine, you can play any drum sound by (press) the right button.
2   You can create drum music without (play) a drum.
3   What we hear as sound are (change) in air pressure.
4   These are converted to electrical signals by (use) a microphone.
5   The information contained in the drum machine memory consists of (sample) of these electrical signals.
6   A drum machine contains (record) of sound taken at measured intervals.
7   This process is called (sample).
8   The functions of a drum machine include (pan) and (tune).
9   Panning means the (position) of the drum sound in stereo.

Word study   *Compound nouns, 1*

Study these examples of compound nouns and their meanings:

a silicon diode = a diode which contains silicon
a smoke alarm = an alarm which warns of smoke
a car radio   = a radio for use in a car

Task 6   Explain each of these compounds:

1   a burglar alarm
2   a clock timer
3   a mercury switch
4   a car phone
5   a germanium diode
6   a ground wave
7   a block diagram
8   an assembly line

Some compound nouns have become single words, for example, *a voltmeter* – an instrument for measuring voltage. Explain the meaning of these words:

9   a fuseholder
10   a wavemeter
11   a cellphone
12   headphones
13   an ammeter
14   a handset

Technical reading *Sampling*

Task 7

Read the text and answer these questions:

1. Is a sine wave an example of an analogue wave or a digital wave?
2. How many voltage levels does a digital signal have?
3. What is an ADC?
4. How frequently must an analogue signal be sampled when converting it to a digital signal?
5. What term means a 'binary digit'?
6. What effect do rounding errors have on a signal when it is converted back to an analogue form?

The magnitude of an analogue signal varies gradually with time over a range of values. Fig. 1 shows an analogue signal in the shape of a sine wave.

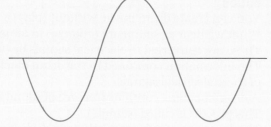

Fig. 1

5 Modern electronic circuits, however, often use digital signals because they can be processed more easily. The magnitude of a digital signal has only two levels, high and low, which can be represented by the binary digits 1 and 0 respectively (see Fig. 2).

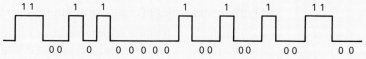

Fig. 2

The analogue signals produced by transducers can be changed into digital signals using an analogue-to-digital converter (ADC).

10 Because the analogue signal is constantly varying, samples of the original signal must be taken at successive intervals of time. The magnitudes of the samples are changed into digital values by the ADC. This process is known as sampling (see Fig. 3).

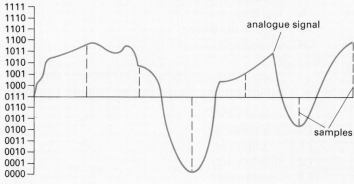

Fig. 3

The higher the frequency of the analogue signal, the more often it
must be sampled. However, it is usually adequate to sample a signal
at twice its highest frequency.

Each binary digit used to show a binary value is known as a bit. The
accuracy of conversion is limited by the number of binary bits used by
the ADC. If the conversion is made using a four-bit ADC, only sixteen
different binary values can be produced. The smallest value is 0000
and the largest is 1111. If an 8-bit ADC is used, then 256 (2^8) different
digital values can be produced. When a measurement of the analogue
signal does not coincide with one of these binary values, it must be
rounded up or down (see Fig. 4).

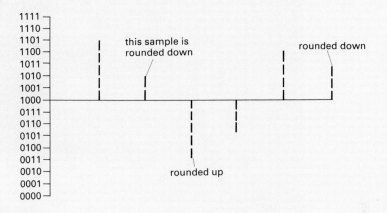

Fig. 4

This leads to inaccuracies in the digital measurements. If the resulting
digital signal is converted back to an analogue signal using a digital-
to-analogue converter (DAC), these rounding errors will cause the
analogue signal to suffer some distortion as shown in Fig. 5.

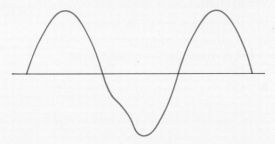

Fig. 5

Although low-quality transmission systems such as digital telephone
networks can operate successfully using 8-bit ADCs, it is necessary to
use 12, 14, or 16-bit ADCs in high quality music systems.

16 Audio recording systems

Tuning-in

Task 1   Try to answer these questions:

1   What problems are there with records?
2   What other recording systems are there?
3   What do these abbreviations mean?
   a   LP
   b   CD

Task 2   Read quickly through this text to check your answers to Task 1.

Audio recording systems

For a long time hi-fi recordings have been produced on vinyl gramophone records. Records use an analogue recording system, which stores patterns by cutting a continuous groove in a vinyl disk. The shape of the sides of the groove represents the audio pattern. The
5   sound can be reproduced by spinning the record and using the movement of a metal needle in the groove to produce varying magnetic fields (see Fig. 1). These magnetic fields are then processed to produce the sound. A typical LP (long-playing record) has a recording capacity of about 45 minutes.

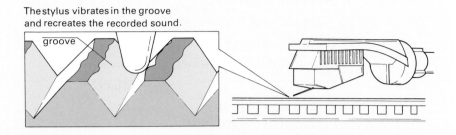

The stylus vibrates in the groove and recreates the recorded sound.

groove

Fig. 1

10 A digital recording system, known as a compact disc (CD) system, was introduced in 1982. This uses a laser optical mechanism in which a laser beam reads marks on the surface of a specially prepared perspex disc. It gives near-perfect reproduction of sound and the sound quality does not deteriorate with use. Some of the problems associated with
15 vinyl records are eliminated such as 'crackle' caused by dust and static, and 'jumping', due to scratches on the recording surface.

In a CD system, a recording is made by electronically sampling the sound 44,100 times every second. The electronic samples are used to control a laser beam, which makes a pattern of very small pits in the
20 surface of the perspex disc. The audio pattern is represented by the length of the pits and the distance between them. The pits are arranged in circular tracks. A typical CD has about 20,000 circular tracks and a maximum recording capacity of 74 minutes.

To play back the recording, the disc is made to revolve at a constant
25 speed and a laser beam is directed at its surface. The varying reflection of the laser beam is fed into a digital-to-analogue converter (DAC). This produces the electronic signals, which are amplified to drive a loudspeaker.

Task 3

Use the text above to complete this table of differences between LPs and CDs:

		LPs	CDs
1	Recording system	analogue	
2	Sound quality	poorer than the original	
3	Access	serial	random
4	Audio pattern		pits
5	Material		perspex
6	Playing mechanism	mechanical	
7	Durability	easily damaged	
8	Size	12 inches	12cm
9	Playing time		

Language study *Cause and effect, 1*

Study this sentence:

> *Dust on records causes crackle.*

It contains a cause and an effect. Identify them.

We can link a cause and effect as follows:

Cause		**Effect**
Dust on records	*causes* *leads to* *results in* *is the cause of*	*crackle.*

We can also put the effect first:

Effect		**Cause**
Crackle	*is caused by* *results from* *is the effect of* *is due to*	*dust on records.*

Task 4

Items in List 1 can be causes or effects of items in List 2. Match the pairs. Compare your answers with your partner. For example:

> *mains frequency interference*   *hum*

	List 1		**List 2**
1	distortion	**a**	interference on radios
2	noise generated within components	**b**	too high a recording level
		c	the tape rubbing against the head
3	overheating a transistor	**d**	scratches on records
4	dirty heads	**e**	hiss
5	a build-up of oxide on the head	**f**	damage
6	jumping	**g**	poor recordings
7	unwanted signals		

Task 5

Write sentences to show the relationship between the pairs you linked in Task 4. For example:

> *Mains frequency interference results in hum.*

Speaking practice

Task 6

Work in pairs, **A** and **B**.

Student A: Read the text on page 177 to find out about DCCs.
Student B: Read the text on page 184 to find out about MDs.

Complete your section of the table at the top of the following page. Then find out enough information from your partner to complete the other section of the table. When you have finished, read each other's texts to check you have completed the table correctly.

Ask questions like these:

> *What recording system do MDs use?*
> *What's the sound quality like?*

		DCC	MD
1	Recording system		
2	Sound quality		
3	Access		
4	Medium		
5	Playing time		
6	Advantages		

Writing *Linking facts and ideas, 3*

Task 7

Study this diagram, which explains the operation of automatic doors. Then turn to the next page and link each set of statements using words or phrases of your own to make your own explanation. Omit unnecessary words and make any other changes required.

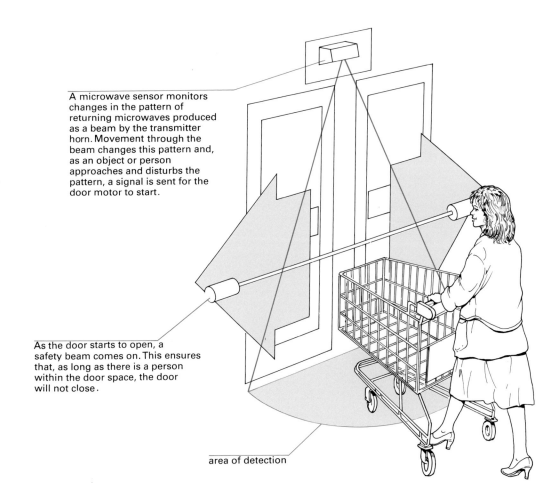

A microwave sensor monitors changes in the pattern of returning microwaves produced as a beam by the transmitter horn. Movement through the beam changes this pattern and, as an object or person approaches and disturbs the pattern, a signal is sent for the door motor to start.

As the door starts to open, a safety beam comes on. This ensures that, as long as there is a person within the door space, the door will not close.

area of detection

1   Automatic doors are used in places such as airports, supermarkets, and hospitals.
    Traditional doors would be a nuisance in these places.

2   Automatic doors are fitted with a microwave sensor.
    The sensor detects movement.

3   The doors are switched on.
    A microwave transmitter sends out a microwave beam.

4   The beam is in a semicircular pattern.
    The doors open when you approach from any angle.

5   The microwaves are reflected back to the sensor.
    The reflected microwaves are analysed by a microprocessor.

6   A person or object moves towards the doors.
    The waves are reflected back to the sensor at a different frequency.

7   The microprocessor detects this change.
    The microprocessor instructs the motor to open the doors.

8   The doors are fitted with a time-delay mechanism.
    The doors remain open for about four seconds before closing again.

9   A person remains standing in the doorway.
    A safety beam prevents the doors from closing.

17 CDs

Listening

Sales of LPs are falling very quickly in the UK. In 1992, one major supplier of popular music announced that it would no longer sell LPs. However, specialist shops continue to stock vinyl records and some music lovers prefer them to other forms of recording. On this tape, you will hear an expert giving his opinion on which form of recording is better: LPs or CDs.

Task 1   As you listen, answer these questions:

1 Why do some people prefer LPs?
2 What is the expert's choice?
3 What are the advantages of CDs?
4 What is the difference between analogue and digital recording?
5 Why does digital recording produce better quality sound?
6 What disadvantages of CDs does he give?
7 What does he mean by marketing?
8 What might be the effect of so many people having CD players?
9 Which audio system does he favour?
10 What's his longterm forecast?
11 What would be the advantage of such a system?

Task 2   Here is the completed table of differences from Unit 16. Listen again to the tape. Tick the differences the expert mentions.

		LPs	CDs
1	Recording system	analogue	digital
2	Sound quality	poorer than the original	like the original
3	Access	serial	random
4	Audio pattern	grooves	pits
5	Material	vinyl	perspex
6	Playing mechanism	mechanical	laser
7	Durability	easily damaged	does not deteriorate
8	Size	12 inches	12cm
9	Playing time	45 minutes	74 minutes

Language study   *Comparison and contrast, 2*

In Unit 2, we studied some ways of describing similarities and differences in English. In this unit we will examine some other ways to describe differences: to make contrasts.

On the tape the expert contrasted:

1   LPs and CDs
2   analogue and digital recording
3   CDs and newer systems

Here are some of the things he said:

*They (CDs) use laser light **rather than** a needle.*
*LPs are analogue recordings **while** CDs are digital.*
*It (an analogue signal) can have any value . . . **but** in digital the signal is either on or off.*
*You can process a digital signal **with greater accuracy than** a constantly varying signal.*

Here are some other expressions used to make contrasts:

    differ from   *is/are different from*   *in contrast to*   *whereas*   *unlike*

Task 3   Look back at the table of differences in Task 2. Contrast LPs and CDs for each point in the table. Use the expressions from the examples listed above. For example:

    1   *Unlike LPs, CDs use a digital recording system.*

18 Graphs

Reading *Understanding graphs*

In electronics, graphs are a common way of giving information. They allow a great deal of data to be presented easily in visual form. Mostly this information is technical, but we start with a non-technical example.

Task 1

This graph shows the sales of singles in the UK over a seven-year period some time ago. This was a period of considerable change in people's choice of format when buying recorded music.

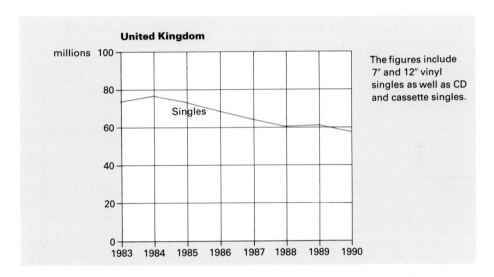

The figures include 7″ and 12″ vinyl singles as well as CD and cassette singles.

Write a sentence to describe sales for these periods:

1 1983–1984 _____

2 1986–1988 _____

3 1988–1989 _____

Language study *Describing graphs*

Look at the period 1983–1984 on the graph. We can describe sales of singles in two ways:

1 *Sales of singles* **rose**.
2 *There* **was a rise** *in the sales of singles.*

We can make our description more accurate like this:

3 *Sales of singles* **rose slightly**.
4 *There* **was a slight rise** *in the sales of singles.*

Study this table of verbs and related nouns of change. The past form of irregular verbs is given in brackets.

Direction	Verb	Noun
Up	climb go up (went up) increase rise (rose)	increase rise
Down	decline decrease dip drop fall (fell) go down (went down)	decline decrease dip drop fall
Level	not change remain constant	no change

These adjectives and adverbs are used to describe the rate of change:

Adjective	Adverb
slight	slightly
gradual	gradually
steady	steadily
steep	steeply
sharp	sharply
sudden	suddenly
fast	fast

Task 2

Study this graph, which compares the sales of LPs, cassettes, CDs, and singles over the same seven-year period.

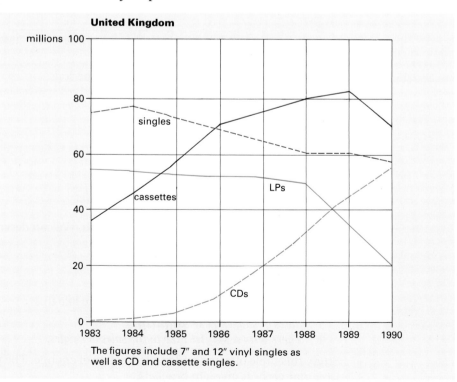

The figures include 7″ and 12″ vinyl singles as well as CD and cassette singles.

Write a sentence to describe sales for these periods:

1 Cassettes 1983–1986 _____

2 Cassettes 1989–1990 _____

3 LPs 1983–1988 _____

4 LPs 1988–1990 _____

5 CDs 1983–1984 _____

6 CDs 1984–1985 _____

7 CDs 1985–1986 _____

8 CDs 1986–1990 _____

Task 3

Make comparisons of sales of different products for these periods. For example:

CDs and singles 1986–1988

Sales of CDs rose steeply, **but**/**while** *sales of singles fell steadily.*
As *sales of CDs rose, sales of singles fell.*

1 CDs and LPs 1986–1988 _____

_____

2 CDs and cassettes 1986–1988 _____

_____

3 Singles and CDs 1983–1984 _____

_____

4 Cassettes and LPs 1983–1986 _____

_____

5 Singles and LPs 1989–1990 _____

_____

Task 4

Try to explain the changes on the graph. List your reasons. Then compare your ideas with this text:

> In 1989, sales of compact discs (CDs) exceeded sales of long-play albums (LPs) for the first time. By 1990, CD sales were more than double those of LPs. Cheaper CD players and the introduction of mid-price and budget-price discs have been partly responsible for the
> 5 increase in CD sales.
>
> Sales of LPs fell by 35 per cent between 1989 and 1990 to less than 25 million, and cassette sales also fell. Despite this, cassettes still accounted for over a third of all items sold. Their continued popularity is partially due to the increase in ownership of personal stereos.

Word study *Common verbs in electronics*

Task 5

These verbs are often used in electronics:

conduct   emit   rectify   sample
dissipate   process   record   suppress

Fill in the gaps in these sentences with an appropriate verb from the list above. Make sure the verb is in the correct form.

1 Computers _____ data.

2 You can _____ sound on tape or disc.

3 A bridge circuit is used to _____ alternating current to produce direct current.

4 All metals, and some non-metals such as carbon, _____ electricity.

5 To prevent radio interference, you must _____ any sources of interference such as car ignition systems.

6 Power transistors _____ heat. Therefore they must be mounted on a heatsink.

7 The electron gun in a CRT _____ a stream of electrons.

8 When recording a CD, sound is _____ 44,100 times every second.

Writing *Describing graphs*

Task 6

Study this graph which shows what happens when a voltage is applied across a silicon PN junction diode.

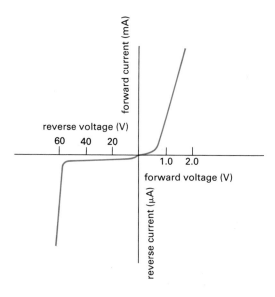

100

Now complete the spaces in this text with reference to the graph. Each space represents several missing words.

The first quadrant shows the characteristics of the diode when it is forward biased. When the voltage is increased, at first the current [1]_____ When the voltage reaches about 600mV there is [2]_____. The current continues to rise as [3]_____ but eventually a point is reached where the diode would be destroyed by heat.

The third quadrant shows what happens when the diode is reverse biased. There is almost no [4]_____. The diode is therefore a good rectifier. It conducts well in one direction and almost not at all in the other. However, there is [5]_____ reverse current. This leakage current [6]_____ until what is known as breakdown voltage. At this point there is [7]_____ in the reverse current. This sudden increase is called the Zener effect.

Speaking practice

Task 7

Work in pairs, **A** and **B**. Give your partner sufficient information about your graph so that he or she can sketch it. When you have finished, compare the graphs you have drawn with the originals.

Student A: Your graph is on page 178.
Student B: Your graph is on page 185.

19 Test and repair instruments

Tuning-in

Task 1

List as many instruments used for testing and repair in electronics as you can. Compare your list with that of another group.

Task 2

How many of these instruments can you identify? Can you explain their use?

1

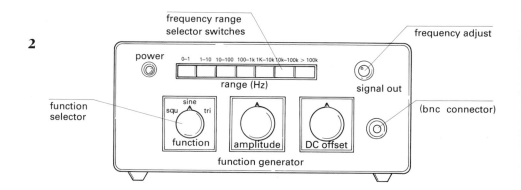

probe

red LED

green LED

powered by circuit under test

2

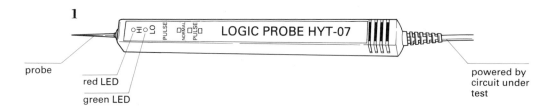

frequency range selector switches

frequency adjust

power

range (Hz)

signal out

function selector

function

amplitude

DC offset

(bnc connector)

function generator

3   **4**

Task 3   Check your answers to Tasks 1 and 2 by reading this text:

> The following instruments are commonly used for the test and repair
> of electronic circuits.
>
> **Multimeter**
> This instrument can be used to measure a number of different
> electrical quantities, such as voltage, current, and resistance, i.e. it is a
> 5 combined voltmeter, ammeter, and ohmmeter. Multimeters can have
> analogue or digital displays and can be switched to different
> measuring ranges.
>
> **Logic probe**
> This instrument is used for measuring voltage levels and pulses in
> digital logic circuits. When the probe is placed on the pin of a logic IC,
> 10 small coloured LEDs light up to indicate if a pulse is detected or
> whether the pin is at a high or a low logic level.
>
> **Oscilloscope**
> This instrument is used to measure fast-moving signals. It shows how
> a signal varies with time or relative to another signal. It uses a cathode
> ray tube to display the waveform of the measured signal on a screen.
>
> **Function generator**
> 15 This instrument contains a triangular wave oscillator which can be
> switched to produce triangular, square, or sine waves over a range of
> frequencies. It is used to test and adjust a variety of electronic
> equipment such as audio amplifiers. The function generator provides
> a known signal which can be injected into a circuit. Often it is used
> 20 with an oscilloscope so that a visual display of the waveform can be
> seen.

Task 4   Which of the instruments would you use to do the following?

1 to check a fuse
2 to determine the frequency response of an audio amplifier
3 to test for the presence of a control signal on the output pin of a computer chip
4 to determine the value of the current through a transformer
5 to measure the frequency of an oscillator

Reading *Information transfer*

The task which follows provides further practice in combining information from a diagram and a text when reading.

Task 5

With the help of this diagram, complete the gaps in the text.

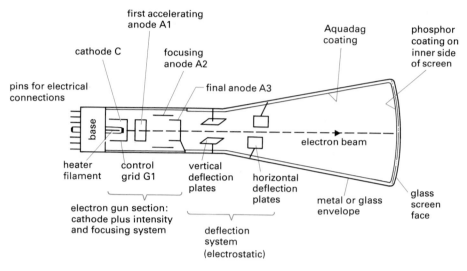

CRT construction

Fig. 1

Cathode ray tube

Televisions as well as computers, radar systems, and oscilloscopes use a cathode ray tube (CRT) to produce an output display. The construction and operation of the CRT is similar in each case but the simplest type of CRT is found in oscilloscopes.

A CRT is really a large vacuum tube valve. It has [1]_____ main sections. The first section is an electron [2]_____ which emits a stream of electrons. The electron gun contains an electron lens which [3]_____ the electrons into a narrow electron [4]_____.

The second section is a [5]_____ system, which allows the beam to be moved [6]_____ or horizontally. Oscilloscopes use charged metal [7]_____ to give [8]_____ deflection, whereas television sets use electromagnetic coils to give electromagnetic [9]_____.

The last section is a screen with a [10]_____ coating. The electron beam hits the screen, making the phosphor glow and causing a spot to be displayed. The colour of the spot depends on the type of phosphor used.

Language study *Cause and effect, 2*

Study these statements:

1   *The electron beam hits the screen.*
2   *The phosphor glows.*

Why does the phosphor glow? What is the relationship between statement (1) and (2)?

Statement (1) is a *cause* and statement (2) is an *effect*. We can link cause and effect statements in a number of ways. Study these ways, which use *cause* and *make*.

The electron beam hits the screen **causing** *the phosphor to glow.*

The electron beam hits the screen **making** *the phosphor glow.*

Now study these cause and effect statements:

3   *The phosphor glows.*
4   *A spot is displayed.*

The effect is in the passive. We can link cause and effect like this:

The phosphor glows **causing** *a spot* **to be** *display***ed***.*

Task 6

Link each of these cause and effect statements to make one sentence:

1   **a**   A magnetic field is set up in the speaker coil.
    b   The coil vibrates.

2   **a**   The coil pushes and pulls the speaker cone.
    b   Sound waves are produced.

3   **a**   A voltage is applied to a quartz crystal.
    b   The quartz crystal expands and contracts.

4   **a**   A voltage is applied to the Y-plates.
    b   The electron beam is deflected.

5   **a**   Current flows through the filament.
    b   The heater glows.

Word Study *Compound nouns, 2*

Task 7

Study these examples of compound nouns:

   a signal generator = equipment for generating signals
   a cassette player = equipment for playing cassettes
   a battery tester = equipment for testing batteries

What do we call equipment for . . .

1   playing CDs?
2   receiving radio (signals)?
3   charging batteries?
4   amplifying aerial (signals)?
5   filtering (out) noise?
6   synthesizing speech?
7   cleaning cassette heads?
8   amplifying (the) power (of a signal)?
9   sensing vibration?
10 scanning (the human) body (for disease)?

Technical reading *Cathode ray oscilloscope*

Task 8

Work in groups of three: **A**, **B**, and **C**.

Student A: Read *Electron gun* and take notes.
Student B: Read *Deflection system* and take notes.
Student C: Read *Phosphor screen* and take notes.

Using your notes and Fig. 1 on page 104, explain to the others in your group how your section of the CRT works. **A** should start. **B** may use Fig. 2 as part of the explanation.

Electron gun

para

A stream of electrons is released from the surface of the cathode (C)   1
when it is heated by the heater filament. The electrons are
accelerated towards the screen by a set of three positively-charged
cylindrical anodes (A1, A2, A3). Each anode has a higher charge
5 than the one before. As the electrons move towards the anodes,
they pass through a hole in a negatively-charged metal disc. This
disc is known as the control grid. By adjusting the intensity control
on the oscilloscope, the charge on the grid can be varied. This
allows the number of electrons reaching the screen, and therefore
10 the brilliance or brightness of the spot on the screen, to be adjusted.

The three anodes form the electron lens. The oscilloscope focus   2
control allows the voltage on the second anode (A2) to be varied
and causes the stream of electrons to be focused into a narrow
beam. If the oscilloscope has an astigmatism control, it is used to
15 vary the voltage on the third anode (A3). This allows the shape of
the spot on the screen to be adjusted to make it perfectly round.

Deflection system

After leaving the electron gun, the electron beam is deflected by   3
two pairs of parallel metal plates. The pairs of deflection plates are
situated at right angles to each other.

20 The signal to be measured is amplified by the Y-amplifier in the   4
oscilloscope, then applied to the first set of deflection plates, known
as the Y-plates. This causes the electron beam to be deflected
vertically in proportion to the magnitude of the input signal.

The oscilloscope has a timebase generator which produces a   5
25 sawtooth wave output as shown in Fig. 2.

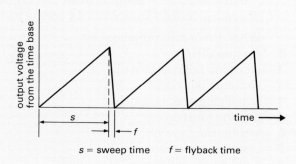

s = sweep time   *f* = flyback time

Fig. 2.

This is fed into the X-amplifier of the oscilloscope, then applied to   6
the second set of deflection plates, known as the X-plates. This
causes the electron beam to be deflected in the horizontal direction
in such a way that the spot moves from left to right across the
30 screen at a steady rate. When it reaches the right side of the screen,
it rapidly returns to the left side again. This allows the screen to
show how the measured signal varies with time.

Phosphor screen

The X and Y deflections of the electron beam cause the signal being   7
measured to be displayed in the form of a wave, with the
35 magnitude of the signal being given on the vertical axis and the
time variation on the horizontal axis. A piece of transparent plastic
known as a graticule is attached to the front of the screen. This has
a grid of horizontal and vertical lines marked on it and allows
accurate measurements of the signal to be made.

40 A large build-up of negative charge could be caused by the electron   8
beam hitting the phosphor screen. To help prevent this, the inside
of the CRT, between the deflection system and the screen, is coated
with a carbon compound known as Aquadag. This is attached to the
high voltage anode (A3) to provide an escape path for the excess
45 electrons.

The CRT is enclosed in a metal casing made from an alloy of nickel,   9
known as mu-metal. This has a very high magnetic permeability
and prevents external magnetic fields from causing unwanted
beam deflections.

20 High definition television

Tuning-in

Task 1

Carry out a survey to find out the viewing habits of your class and their ideas on future developments in television. You may add extra questions of your own.

1   How many hours of television do you watch each week?
2   When do you watch television?
3   What sort of programmes do you watch?
4   Which television station do you watch most/least often?
5   How do you think television will change in the future?

Compare viewing habits for your class with the viewing habits of people of your own age group in the UK. Are there any differences?

United Kingdom

Age groups	Television viewing (hours/mins per week)				
	1984	1985	1986	1987	1988
4–15 years	16:10	19:59	20:35	19:14	18:34
16–34 years	18:16	21:36	21:10	20:03	20:36
35–64 years	23:24	28:04	27:49	27:25	27:17
65 years and over	29:50	36:35	36:55	37:41	37:25
All aged 4 years and over	23:03	26:33	25:54	25:25	25:21

Task 2 Study these graphics. Note ways in which high definition television will be different from existing sets. Compare your answers with your partner. For example:

Feature	Existing	High definition
no. of lines	625	1,250

The aim of high definition television (HDTV) is to provide the viewer with more realistic images than are offered by today's television sets.

a

b

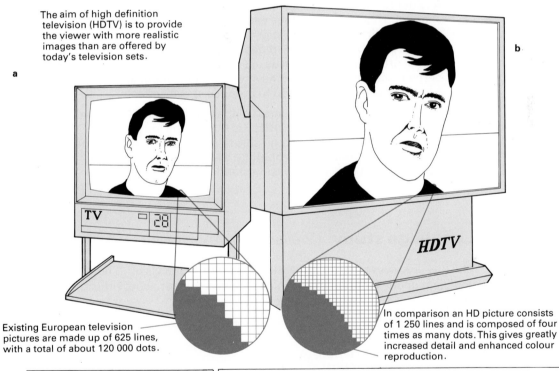

Existing European television pictures are made up of 625 lines, with a total of about 120 000 dots.

In comparison an HD picture consists of 1 250 lines and is composed of four times as many dots. This gives greatly increased detail and enhanced colour reproduction.

c

For HDTV the width/height ratio of the screen has been changed from 4:3 (as in conventional TV) to 16:9, like the screens in cinemas. From corner to corner it measures 100–125 cm.

d Viewing and listening conditions
The optimal viewing distance for HDTV is three times the height of the screen compared with seven times the present televisions.

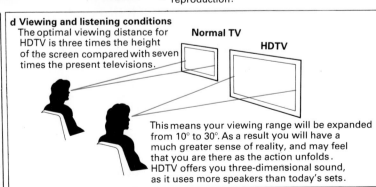

Normal TV

HDTV

This means your viewing range will be expanded from 10° to 30°. As a result you will have a much greater sense of reality, and may feel that you are there as the action unfolds. HDTV offers you three-dimensional sound, as it uses more speakers than today's sets.

Now search this text for further differences to add to your list.

In Europe, the USA, and Japan, the race is on to produce a new generation of television sets. These new sets will be larger than today's models, possibly with 100-centimetre flat screens. Picture quality will be excellent, crisp, and without flicker, as good as those we 5 are used to seeing in the cinema. Sound quality too will be superb, thanks to digital multitrack transmissions. By the turn of the century such sets may be offering programmes in a choice of languages as they will be equipped with eight sound tracks.

In Europe, the term HDTV is used. In the USA, the more generic term 10 ATV, Advanced Television, has been adopted. The Japanese, who were the first to start work on the new technology, in 1974, called their system Hi-Vision. Whatever name is used, these new sets share certain features.

The picture is displayed using more lines per frame. This means that 15 they provide clearer, more detailed, high quality images. The picture can be displayed on large, wide screens which are flicker-free. They also provide very high quality three-dimensional sound output.

A wider range of frequencies can be used to transmit each HDTV channel. This is because they can be transmitted at high frequencies 20 which are virtually unused at present. These wide frequency ranges make it possible to transmit digital, rather than analogue signals. Digital processing can then be used in the receivers to provide almost perfect pictures even when the strength of the input signal is low. A computer could also be used to produce special effects.

25 Since not everyone is convinced of the need for such high quality TV systems, the move towards HDTV is likely to be very gradual. The first HDTV receivers will need to be able to process both the old and the new transmissions and, throughout the world, agreement will have to be reached on new transmission standards.

Language study *Certainty*

The text describes possible future developments in television. The writer is confident about some developments and less confident about others. What difference can you see between these statements?

1 *By the turn of the century such sets* **may** *be offering programmes in a choice of languages.*
2 *Picture quality* **will** *be excellent.*
3 *The move towards HDTV is* **likely** *to be very gradual.*

We cannot measure certainty in language with precision, but the following table provides a guide to how certain a writer is about a future development.

Certainty (%)	Verb	Adjective	Adverb
100	will	certain	certainly
85		likely	unlikely
75		probable	probably
		improbable	
50	could/may	possible	possibly

Task 4 📺 Listen to this expert on audio systems, recorded in 1992. Note his predictions for each format and the certainty expressions he uses. Do you share his views? Has the situation changed today? Discuss in groups.

	Prediction	Certainty expressions
LPs		
Cassettes		
MDs		
CDs		

Task 5 How likely are these developments in the next five years? Make statements about each development using the certainty expressions in the table on page 110. Compare your answers. The graph on page 98 may help you with some of the statements. For example:

> Most houses in your country will be cleaned by electronic robots.
>
> *I think it's unlikely that most houses in my country will be cleaned by electronic robots. It's possible that some houses will use them.*

1 Vinyl records will not be made.

2 Ordinary audio cassettes will not be made.

3 Most families in your country will have CD players.

4 Most families in your country will have MD players.

5 Most families in your country will have DCC players.

6 Computers will understand and respond to your spoken language.

7 Cars will be electronically guided through cities.

8 Most teaching will be done by computers.

9 No manual labour will be done in factories in your country.

10 Most families in your country will have HDTVs.

Technical reading *Television display*

Task 6 Find the answers to these questions by studying the text and diagrams on the following page.

1 What controls the movement of the spot of light across a television screen?

2 What name is given to the rapid movement of the spot back across the screen to the start of the next line?

3 How many lines are used to build up a frame in present European television systems?

4 What happens to a screen if the frame is not scanned at least forty times per second?

Television pictures

A television picture is built up gradually by moving a spot of light across and down a screen in a raster pattern (see Fig. 1).

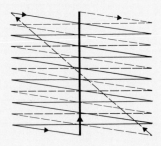

Fig. 1

The video signal causes the brightness of the spot to vary in proportion to the intensity of light in the original image. The
5 movement of the spot across the screen is controlled by the line scan signal. Each time the spot reaches the right side of the screen, it is blanked and moved rapidly back to the left side ready to start the next line. This rapid movement back to a starting position is known as flyback. Each complete image or frame requires a minimum of 500
10 lines to give a picture of acceptable quality. The present European TV system uses 625 lines per frame.

The movement of the spot down the screen is controlled by the field scan signal. When the spot reaches the bottom of the screen, it is blanked and moved rapidly back to the top of the screen. The frame
15 must be scanned at least forty times per second to prevent the screen from flickering. The present European TV system has a frame scan rate of 50Hz.

The video signal contains line and field sync pulses to make sure that the TV receiver starts a new line and a new frame at the same time as
20 the TV camera (see Fig. 2).

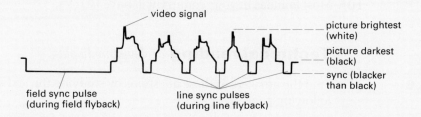

Fig. 2

To allow the video signal to be transmitted using a smaller range of frequencies, each frame is transmitted in two separate halves, known as fields. The first time the spot travels down the screen it displays the first field, which consists of the odd-numbered frame lines. The
25 second time the spot travels down the screen it displays the second field, which consists of the even-numbered frame lines. Combining two fields in this way is known as interlacing. Although the fields are displayed one after the other, it happens so quickly that the human eye sees them as one complete picture.

Writing *Linking facts and ideas, 4*

Task 7
Link each set of statements, using words or phrases of your own to make an explanation of how a television picture is composed. Omit unnecessary words and make any other changes required.

1 A television picture is built up gradually.
This is done by a moving spot.

2 The spot strikes the television screen.
The phosphor coating on the screen emits light.
The light varies in brightness according to the intensity of the original image.

3 The spot reaches the right side of the screen.
The spot is blanked.
The spot is moved rapidly back to the left side in a movement called flyback.

4 The present European system sweeps the screen in a series of lines.
There are 625 closely-spaced lines.
Using 625 lines ensures a good quality picture.

5 The movement across the screen is controlled by the line scan signal.
The movement down the screen is controlled by the field scan signal.

6 The scan rate must be greater than 40Hz.
A lower scan rate would cause the screen to flicker.

7 Sync pulses are added to the video signal.
The sync pulses ensure that the TV camera and TV receiver start a new line and frame at the same time.

8 The build-up of the screen happens so quickly.
The eye sees only a complete picture.

Task 8
Now divide your completed statements into two paragraphs. Give your text a suitable title.

21 Video cassette recorder

Tuning-in

Task 1

Read this newspaper article:

High-tech mystery

High-tech machines leave many owners baffled, according to a survey by electrical retailers. Nearly a third of those with video recorders and 57 per cent of camcorder owners do not use all the functions. The 16-24 age group understood the technology best, with 70 per cent saying they were the family expert.

A recent survey of video owners found that over 70% could not set their timers

Survey your group. Ask these questions:

1 Does your family have a VCR?
2 What is it used for?
3 Who knows how to set the timer?
4 Does your family have a camcorder?
5 What functions are not used?

Task 2

You are going to hear a short talk. The speaker will explain some of the differences between conventional audio and video recording. Before you listen, note down any differences you already know.

Task 3

Now listen and complete this table to show some of the differences between audio and video recording.

	Audio	**Video**
Medium	magnetic tape	magnetic tape
Tape width	¼ inch	_____
Type of heads	_____	_____
Speed (cm/sec)	_____	2.339 (VHS)
Scanning	linear	_____
Data recorded in 1 sec.	_____	25 complete separate pictures

Task 4

Read this text and match each change in VCR design with its result, as in the example below.

The step from recording sound on magnetic tape to doing the same with video signals is one of increased band width. Early reel-to-reel machines used one-inch wide tape and made the most of the available band width by moving the tape past the head at high speed.
5   Unfortunately, this meant that the transport mechanism had to be built to a high specification.

Improvements in magnetic tape and the use of helical scanning meant that far more data could be crammed into a smaller area. By spinning the head at a high speed, the rate at which the data could be stored or
10   retrieved was increased. Aligning the head at an angle to the tape laid down the information as a series of slanted tracks. This allowed the cassette tape to be narrower and move at a slower speed, giving rise to the modern video cassette recorder.

Early VCRs were playback-only, but by building in a full-colour TV
15   tuner, programmes could be recorded from the air while another channel was being viewed on a normal TV. The inclusion of a timer meant that recordings could be made and viewed at a later date. Early timers only switched the tape on at a certain time, leaving the VCR running until the tape finished. The latest machines allow a large
20   number of on/off programmed times to be set so that viewers can go on holiday and not miss a single episode of their favourite soap opera.

	Design change		Result
Example	*moving the tape past the head at high speed*		*The transport mechanism had to be built to a high specification.*
1	improvements in magnetic tape and the use of helical scanning	a	The information was laid down as a series of slanted tracks.
2	spinning the head at a high speed	b	The modern VCR could be produced.
3	aligning the head at an angle to the tape	c	Far more data could be crammed into a smaller area.
4	recording information in slanted tracks	d	Recordings could be made and viewed at a later date.
5	all these improvements	e	The rate at which the data could be stored or retrieved was increased.
6	the inclusion of a timer	f	The cassette tape could be narrower and the tape could move at a slower speed.

Language study   *Change and result*

Study this design change and its result:

spinning the head at a high speed	*The rate at which the data could be stored or retrieved was increased.*

We can link a change and its consequence in two ways:

1 *Spinning the head at a high speed* **meant that** *the rate at which the data could be stored or retrieved was increased.*

2 **As a result of** *spinning the head at a high speed, the rate at which the data could be stored or retrieved was increased.*

We can use these methods when the change is a noun or a noun phrase.

Task 5

Link the other changes and results in Task 4, using both these methods.

Task 6

Label the numbers in the diagram on the following page using the terms in italics from the text below. One has been done for you.

> ### The transport mechanism
>
> Out of the machine, the reels of a VHS tape are locked and the tape is covered by a flap. Once in the machine, the reels become unlocked and the tape guard lifts up to expose the tape. Pressing the play or record buttons causes the *tape-loading rollers* to pull a length of tape
> 5 from the cassette and wrap it around the *head drum*. *Guide rollers* then steer the tape from the *feed reel* to the *take-up reel* and information is transferred to or from the tape. On most machines audio information is transferred via a static *audio head* which puts information on a separate track from the video signal – this is one
> 10 reason why an option to record sound separately is generally available.

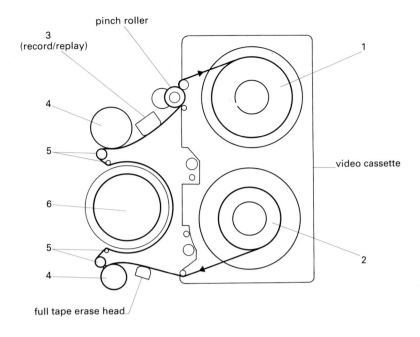

pinch roller

3
(record/replay)

1

4

5

video cassette

6

5

2

4

full tape erase head

Word study *Technical and non-technical words*

Task 7

The talk you listened to in Task 3 contained some less technical language than the texts you have read. Try to match the non-technical words and phrases in List 1 with their technical equivalents in List 2.

List 1 (non-technical)

1 diagonal stripes
2 a fixed head
3 information
4 tilting the drum
5 spinning the heads

List 2 (technical)

a data
b rotating the heads
c a static head
d aligning the head at an angle
e slanted tracks

Speaking practice

Task 8

Work in pairs, **A** and **B**.

Student A: Using the troubleshooting chart on page 179, try to help your partner solve his/her VCR problems. Your own problems are listed on the same chart.

Student B: Using the troubleshooting chart on page 186, try to help your partner solve his/her VCR problems. Your own problems are listed on the same chart.

Useful language:

What's the likely cause?
What should you do if . . . ?
Try . . . -ing.

What's probably wrong with it?
What do I do if . . . ?
It could be that . . .

Writing *Comparing and contrasting, 2*

Task 9

With the help of this diagram and the table you completed in Task 3, compare conventional audio recording and VHS video recording. Describe the similarities and differences. Explain the differences where possible.

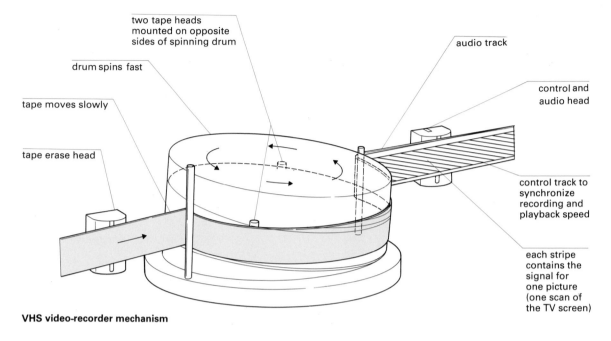

two tape heads mounted on opposite sides of spinning drum

drum spins fast

tape moves slowly

tape erase head

audio track

control and audio head

control track to synchronize recording and playback speed

each stripe contains the signal for one picture (one scan of the TV screen)

VHS video-recorder mechanism

22 Technician

Listening

Peter is a technician at a large college. On the tape he describes his work.

Task 1 As you listen, decide whether these statements are true or false. Then compare answers with your partner.

1 Electronics was Peter's main hobby at school.
2 His father forced him to take up a career in electronics.
3 His first employer did not provide him with training in electronics.
4 Owners can clean their own VCR heads.
5 The rewind motors wear out because the VCR is not being used properly.
6 Sticking broken tapes together with Sellotape is not a good idea.
7 In his present job, Peter finds that operator errors are more common than machine faults.
8 Students sometimes put sandwiches in the VCR machines.
9 Professional cameras allow broadcast-quality tape to be produced.
10 The loss of quality when editing videos is significant.
11 He would like to work for the BBC as a technician.

Now listen again to each section of the tape. This time, listen for detail. Compare answers with your partner.

Part 1

1   What sort of things did Peter make at school?
2   Which company does his father work for?
3   What did the first company that Peter worked for sell?
4   When do rewinding mechanisms start to go wrong?
5   What happens when the plastic drives slip?

Part 2

6   When did he come to the college?
7   What equipment does he maintain?
8   What do students sometimes do with equipment left in the classrooms?

Part 3

9   What equipment does he use to film course material?
10   How is the professional camera different from the domestic camcorder?
11   What do they normally work to when they film a scene?
12   In addition to a recorder and player, what piece of equipment does he use when editing?
13   What quality of tape does he use?
14   What part of his work does he enjoy most?

Reading   *Search reading*

In a number of units you have practised searching a text for specific detail. This involved matching the topic of your search with words in the text. In the task which follows you are asked to find examples of a category: equipment for fault-finding. Before you start your search, think of the kind of examples you may find – tools, instruments, etc. This will help you locate the items more quickly.

Task 3   In this text a service technician describes the equipment required for fault-finding. Make a list of the equipment he mentions.

> For fault-finding you must have at least a multimeter, either analogue or digital. An oscilloscope is not absolutely essential but you will find yourself very restricted without one. It's like trying to repair a car while wearing a blindfold.
>
> 5   For audio equipment, a signal source is needed. Clearly a function generator is useful but simpler and cheaper alternatives work well in most cases. You only need a fixed frequency source, say 400 or 1000 Hz sine or square wave. For cassette recorders a tape with a constant 400Hz wave recorded on both channels is adequate for most fault-
> 10   finding. However, for checking playback levels and frequency response and aligning the tape head, proper test tapes, which are expensive, are required.
>
> For serious work, a collection of test leads and audio connectors is essential. Most modern audio equipment uses phono sockets so it's
> 15   worthwhile investing in cables which terminate in phono plugs. For other types of sockets, adaptors are available.

Task 4   Complete the table of equipment to match each of the necessity expressions.

Equipment	How necessary?
multimeter	must have
_____	is not absolutely essential but you will be very restricted without one
_____	is needed
_____	is useful
_____	is adequate for most fault-finding
_____	are required
_____	is essential

Language study   *Necessity*

Study these ways of showing how necessary something is:

100% positive	*is essential/necessary*
	is needed/required
	you must have
50%	*is useful (but not essential/necessary)*
100% negative	*is not necessary*
	is not needed/required
	you need not have

Task 5   Describe how necessary the following equipment is for fault-finding, according to the service technician. Use appropriate expressions from the list above.

1   multimeter
2   oscilloscope
3   signal source
4   function generator
5   test tapes (for checking levels etc.)
6   test leads and audio connectors

23 Computers

Tuning-in

Task 1

Make a survey of your class to find out how many have access to computers. Use questions like these:

Do you have access to a computer?
Where? At home? At work? At college or university?
What do you use it for?
What kind of computer is it?

You may add other questions of your own.

Task 2

Can you explain what these abbreviations mean?

1 ROM
2 RAM
3 CPU
4 I/O

Check your answers by reading quickly through this text:

Microcomputer systems

The block diagram of a microcomputer system is shown in Fig. 1.

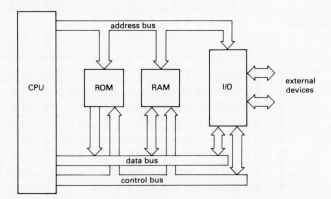

Fig. 1

The I/O (input/output) unit consists of one or more ICs, which are used to control the data going in and out of the computer.

The ROM (read-only memory) and RAM (random-access memory)
5 units consist of a number of special digital logic chips which can store programs and data. The small ROM provides some permanent storage and the RAM is used for temporary storage. Unlike the ROM, the contents of the RAM is constantly changing, but it only operates while the computer is switched on.

10 The CPU (central processing unit) is a microprocessor. It is the main part of the computer, which controls the rest of the system and performs all the arithmetic and logic operations on the data.

Sets of connectors known as buses are used to carry the internal signals between each unit. The data bus is used to transfer data
15 between all the units. The control bus is used to send control signals from the CPU to the other units. The address bus is used to send signals from the CPU which indicate the memory and I/O locations to be used.

Task 3

Fill in the gaps in this table with the help of the text.

Component	Purpose
I/O unit	controls data going in and out of the computer
ROM	_____
_____	temporary storage
_____	controls the system, performs all arithmetic and logic operations on the data
Data bus	_____
Control bus	_____
_____	sends signals from the CPU which indicate the memory and I/O locations to be used

Language study *Describing purpose*

Study these ways of describing the purpose of random access memory:

> RAM **is used for the temporary storage** of programs and data.
> RAM **is used for storing** programs and data temporarily.
> RAM **is used to store** programs and data temporarily.

Task 4

Identify each of the electronic components or pieces of equipment described below. Compare answers with your partner.

1 It's used to change AC voltages from small to large or from large to small.
2 It's used for measuring very small currents.
3 It's used to check the logic levels in the pins of ICS.
4 It's used as part of a burglar alarm to detect movement.
5 It's used for the transmission of RF signals.
6 It's used for protecting circuits from a surge in voltage.
7 It's used to master down different recordings to make a master tape.
8 It's used to find buried metal.

Task 5

Look again at the sentences describing the purpose of RAM. Describe the purpose of each of the other components listed in your completed table in Task 3.

Word study *Prefixes*

Study this term from electronics:

> *semiconductor*

We can divide it into three parts:

> *semi   conduct   or*

Semi is a prefix which means 'half', while *or* is a suffix added to the verb *conduct* to make a noun. From this we can work out that a *semiconductor* is a component which half conducts, i.e. it conducts in one direction only.

Knowledge of common prefixes can help us to work out the meaning of some unfamiliar terms in electronics.

Task 6

Study this table. Try to think of other examples to add. Compare your examples with those of another group.

Explain to the other group the meaning of any terms which they are unfamiliar with.

Prefix	Meaning	Example	Others
de-	reverse the action	decouple	_____
dis-	opposite of	discharge	_____
micro-	small	microchip	_____
multi-	many	multimedia	_____
tele-	far	television	_____
trans-	across	transmitter	_____

Technical reading *Combinational logic*

Task 7   Answer the following questions about the text below.

1   What terms are used in the text for each of the following?
   a   a digital switching circuit
   b   the output of each gate depending on the combination of its inputs
   c   the number of ICs used in a computer
   d   an indication of the number of components used in an IC

2   What is shown by
   a   a truth table?
   b   a pin-out diagram?

3   What is another name for a NOT gate?

4   What are the two common families of logic ICs?

5   What do these abbreviations stand for?
   a   TTL
   b   VLSI
   c   CMOS
   d   MSI

6   Which of these statements are true for CMOS ICs?
   a   They contain bipolar transistors.
   b   They contain field effect transistors.
   c   They are particularly suitable for use in battery-operated portable computers.
   d   They are particularly suitable for use in large, high-speed computers.

para

The decision-making circuits used in modern computers are mainly   1
composed of combinations of digital switching circuits known as
logic gates. Fig. 1 shows the logic symbols and truth tables for
some basic gates.

AND	A	B	out		NAND	A	B	out
	0	0	0			0	0	1
	0	1	0			0	1	1
	1	0	0			1	0	1
	1	1	1			1	1	0

NOT	A	out		OR	A	B	out
	0	1			0	0	0
	1	0			0	1	1
					1	0	1
					1	1	1

Fig. 1

5   The output of each gate depends on the combination of its inputs.   2
This is known as combinational logic. The output for all possible
inputs is shown using a truth table. The truth tables show that the
output of an AND gate is only high (i.e. logic level 1) when all its
inputs are high. The output of a NAND gate, however, stays high
10   unless all its inputs are high. The output of a NOT gate (also known
as an inverter) is always the opposite of its input.

Computers use ICs which contain a number of logic gates on one   3
chip. An IC pin-out diagram shows the arrangement of the gates
and the function of each pin on the chip (see Fig. 2).

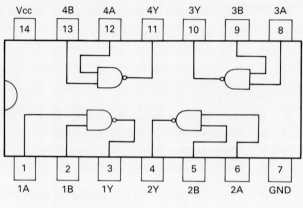

quad 2 input NAND gates
TTL 7400 (CMOS 4011)

Fig. 2

15   The number of ICs used in a computer, i.e. the chip count, can be   4
reduced by connecting NAND gates together to form other types of
gates (see Fig. 3).

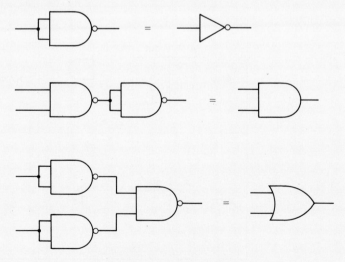

How NAND gates can be used to make basic logic gates

Fig. 3

The number of components in an IC is indicated by its scale of integration as shown in Table 1. The IC shown in Fig. 2 is an SSI
20 device but microprocessors used in computers are VLSI or SLSI devices.

Table 1

Scale of integration	Abbreviation	No. of active components
Small-scale integration	SSI	1 to 10
Medium-scale integration	MSI	10 to 10^2
Large-scale integration	LSI	10^2 to 10^3
Very large-scale integration	VLSI	10^3 to 10^4
Super large-scale integration	SLSI	10^4 to 10^5

There are two common families of logic ICs used in computers. TTL (transistor–transistor logic) ICs use bipolar transistors to form each gate whereas CMOS (complementary metal oxide semiconductor)
25 ICs use field effect transistors (FETs). The different characteristics of each family determine which will be used in a particular computer (see Table 2). For example, TTL ICs are used in large, high-speed computers and CMOS ICs are better for battery-powered portable computers.

Table 2

Properties	TTL	CMOS
Supply voltage	+5V±0.25%	+3V to +15V
Supply current	mA	μA
Power dissipation	mW	μW
Switching speed	fast	relatively slow
Input impedance	low	high

Task 8

Complete these statements with the help of the truth tables in Fig. 1 on page 125. For example, in the case of an AND gate:

a   When A and B are low, *the output is low.*
b   *When A is low and B is high,* the output is low.

1   AND   When A is high and B is low, _____ .

2   NOT   _____ , the output is high.

3   OR   When A and B are high, _____ .

4   NOT   When A is high, _____ .

5   NAND   _____ , the output is low.

6   NAND   When A is high and B is low, _____ .

7   AND   _____ , the output is high.

8   NAND   When A and B are low, _____ .

Writing *Explaining a process control system*

Study this diagram. It shows how an industrial process is controlled using logic gates. With the help of the diagram, complete the blanks in the explanation which follows. Each blank may be one or more words.

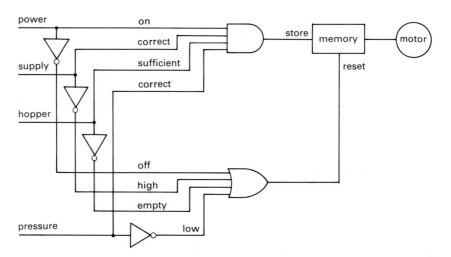

A motor controlling the flow of aluminium blanks to a hydraulic press is switched on only under these conditions:

1   The power is on.

2   The supply voltage is ^{1}_____ .

3   There are ^{2}_____ aluminium blanks in the hopper (store).

4   The ^{3}_____ in the hydraulic press is correct.

Information on these four conditions is fed into an ^{4}_____ as all four conditions must be satisfied for the motor to run. When ^{5}_____ , the output from the AND gate is high. This is fed into the store input of the ^{6}_____ unit to provide a continuous signal to operate the motor.

The motor must stop if any one of these conditions occurs:

1   The power is ^{7}_____ .

2   The ^{8}_____ rises.

3   The hopper is ^{9}_____ .

4   The ^{10}_____ drops.

Information on each of these conditions is fed through a ^{11}_____ . When the input is low, ^{12}_____ . The output from each NOT gate is fed to an ^{13}_____ . When any of the four inputs to the OR gate is high, the output ^{14}_____ . When this is fed to the memory reset, it interrupts the continuous signal to the motor. The motor is switched ^{15}_____ and the flow of aluminium blanks to the press is thus ^{16}_____

24 Digital watch

Tuning-in

Task 1

Study this diagram of a watch. How many functions can you list?

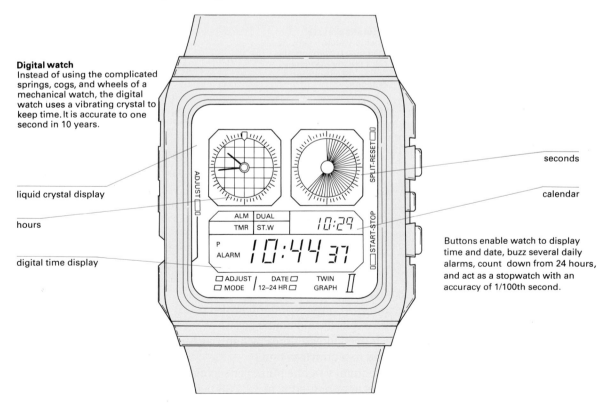

Digital watch
Instead of using the complicated springs, cogs, and wheels of a mechanical watch, the digital watch uses a vibrating crystal to keep time. It is accurate to one second in 10 years.

liquid crystal display

hours

digital time display

ADJUST

ALM | DUAL
TMR | ST.W

P
ALARM

ADJUST / DATE
MODE / 12–24 HR

10:29

10:44 37

TWIN
GRAPH

SPLIT-RESET

START-STOP

seconds

calendar

Buttons enable watch to display time and date, buzz several daily alarms, count down from 24 hours, and act as a stopwatch with an accuracy of 1/100th second.

Task 2

Make a survey of your class to find out how many are wearing digital watches and which functions these watches can display.

Some questions to ask:

Does it show	*the day and date?*
Does it have	*a 12/24-hour option?*
	an alarm?
	a reminder?
Can you use it as	*a stopwatch?*
Does it	*count down from 24 hours, etc.?*

Task 3

Label each step in the flowchart below, which explains how a digital watch works. The first step has been labelled for you.

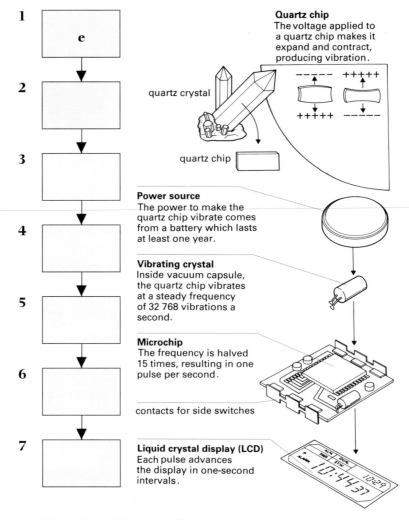

Quartz chip
The voltage applied to a quartz chip makes it expand and contract, producing vibration.

quartz crystal

quartz chip

Power source
The power to make the quartz chip vibrate comes from a battery which lasts at least one year.

Vibrating crystal
Inside vacuum capsule, the quartz chip vibrates at a steady frequency of 32 768 vibrations a second.

Microchip
The frequency is halved 15 times, resulting in one pulse per second.

contacts for side switches

Liquid crystal display (LCD)
Each pulse advances the display in one-second intervals.

a   The pulse is fed to an LCD.
b   The display advances in one-second intervals.
c   The quartz crystal expands and contracts.
d   The frequency is halved fifteen times by a microchip.
e   A voltage is applied to a quartz crystal.
f   This results in a frequency of one pulse per second.
g   The crystal vibrates at a frequency of 32,768 per second.

Read this text to check your answers. Then compare answers with your neighbour.

Digital watch

The traditional mechanical wristwatch uses a balance wheel and hairspring to keep time. In a digital watch these mechanical parts have been replaced by a vibrating quartz crystal controlled by minute electronic circuits.

5 Quartz is a naturally occurring mineral and one of its major sources is Brazil. However, to avoid impurities, the crystals used in watches and clocks are usually created (or 'grown') under controlled conditions. One of the advantages of quartz is that it is very stable.

The artificial quartz crystals used in digital watches are designed to
10 vibrate up to 32,768 cycles per second when the current from a battery is passed through them.

These vibrations produce electric pulses. As the pulses travel through the electronic circuits of the microchip, their rate is gradually halved. The result creates a pulse rate of one per second.

15 Each one-second pulse triggers the microchip to send signals to the digital display to advance the numerals by one second.

The pulses are also used to control different functions such as the hour display, date and alarm signal.

Most modern quartz watches display the time in digits on a liquid
20 crystal display (LCD). This is a thin film of liquid which reacts to electrical charges placed between two sheets of glass. The bottom layer is reflective glass.

Transparent electrical conductors separate the crystals into segments. Each digit is formed from segments — up to seven are normally used.

25 The liquid crystals rearrange their molecules according to whether or not they are charged by electricity.

When the conductors carry no charge, light is reflected out again, so the display will be blank. When the conductors are charged by an electric pulse, the molecules in the charged segments realign and
30 twist the light away from the reflective surface, appearing black. Together, the charged segments therefore appear as figures.

Language Study *Cause and effect, 3*

Here are the statements from Task 3 in the correct sequence. What is the relationship between them?

1 A voltage is applied to a quartz crystal.
2 The quartz crystal expands and contracts.
3 The crystal vibrates at a frequency of 32,768 per second.
4 The frequency is halved fifteen times by a microchip.
5 This results in a frequency of one pulse per second.
6 The pulse is fed to an LCD.
7 The display advances in one-second intervals.

These statements form a cause and effect chain. Note how we can form the links in this chain.

Link 1. In Unit 19, we studied cause and effect links with *make*:

> 1+2   *A voltage is applied to a quartz crystal **making** it expand and contract.*

Link 2. In Unit 12, we studied transitive verbs like *produce*. Often these verbs can be used to form a cause and effect link:

> 1+2+3   *A voltage is applied to a quartz crystal **making** it expand and contract, **producing** vibration at a frequency of 32,768 per second.*

Link 3. In Unit 16, we studied how to use *result in* to link a cause and effect when both are noun phrases. Note how this verb is used here:

> 4+5   *The frequency is halved fifteen times by a microchip **resulting in** a frequency of one pulse per second.*

Link 4. *When* can also link a cause and effect, as in the example which follows. But be careful: one action happening after another does not always indicate that the first action causes the second.

> 6+7   ***When** the pulse is fed to an LCD, it advances the display in one-second intervals.*

We can describe the complete chain as:

> *A voltage is applied to a quartz crystal **making** it expand and contract, **producing** vibration at a frequency of 32,768 per second. The frequency is halved fifteen times by a microchip **resulting in** a frequency of one pulse per second. **When** the pulse is fed to an LCD, it advances the display in one-second intervals.*

Task 5

Study this circuit, which provides a means of monitoring pressure in a system. Changes in pressure trigger a warning.

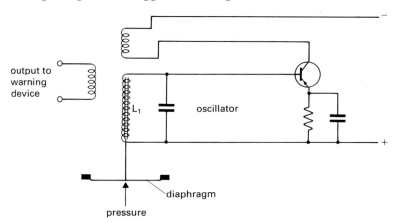

With the help of the circuit, put these steps in the correct sequence to form a cause and effect chain. Then link the steps to make a description of the chain.

a   The diaphragm is pushed out.
b   The oscillator output frequency changes.
c   The pressure increases.
d   The ferrite core rises.
e   The frequency of the tuned circuit changes.
f   The inductance of L_1 alters.
g   There is an audible warning.

Technical reading *Divider circuits*

Task 6

When you have read this text, you should understand:

1   The function of the units which make up the electronics of a digital watch.
2   How dividers work.

Read lines 1–11 quickly and note the names of the units which make up the electronics of the watch. Then read the rest of the text to understand 1 and 2 above.

The electronics of a digital watch may be contained in a single integrated circuit. However, we can think of the chip as a number of separate units, each performing a different function. This can be shown in a block diagram (see Fig. 1).

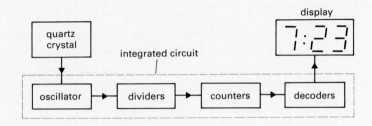

Fig. 1

5 The oscillator generates pulses at a fixed frequency of 32 768Hz. This frequency is determined by the natural oscillation of the quartz crystal. The divider circuits perform binary division on the pulses to reduce their frequency to one pulse per second. A binary count of these pulses is made by the counter circuits and the decoders convert the
10 binary output into signals which light up the appropriate segments of the digital display.

Dividers

Dividers form one of the main components of this system. They consist of circuits which switch between two stable states and are known as bistables or flip-flops (see Fig. 2).

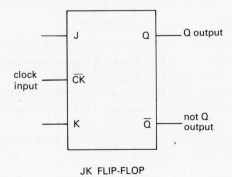

JK FLIP-FLOP

Fig. 2

15 Each time a pulse is applied to the clock input of a flip-flop, its outputs change their logic state from high (logic 1) to low (logic 0) or vice-versa. This means that two clock input pulses cause one pulse to be output from the flip-flop at output Q, as shown in Fig. 3.

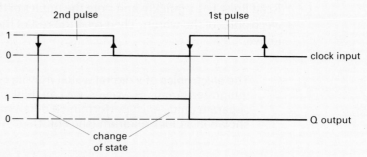

Fig. 3

20 The frequency of the clock input pulse is therefore divided by two at the Q output, i.e. the flip-flop is acting as a binary frequency divider.

If the Q output of the flip-flop is fed into the clock input of another flip-flop, the pulse frequency is again divided by two (see Fig. 4).

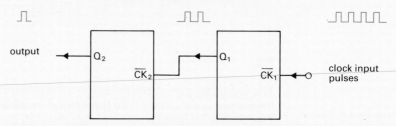

Fig. 4

The output of one flip-flop is connected to the input of the next, i.e. they are connected in cascade. The output frequency at Q_2 is one
25 quarter of the input pulse frequency at CK_1.

The frequency of the oscillator pulse in a digital watch can be reduced from 32 768Hz to 1Hz by using fifteen cascaded flip-flops.

Task 7

Read the text again to match each unit to its function.

Unit		Function
1 oscillator	**a**	divides the frequency 15 times
2 divider	**b**	produces signals to operate the LCD
3 counter	**c**	displays the time
4 decoder	**d**	produces fixed frequency pulses
5 LCD	**e**	makes a binary count of the pulses

Task 8

Take turns at explaining to each other in your group or to your teacher what these terms mean:

1 a flip-flop
2 connected in cascade
3 a bistable circuit
4 logic states

Writing *Linking facts and ideas, 5*

Task 9

Study this diagram which explains the operation of liquid crystal displays. Then link each set of statements using words or phrases of your own to make your own explanation. Omit unnecessary words and make any other changes required.

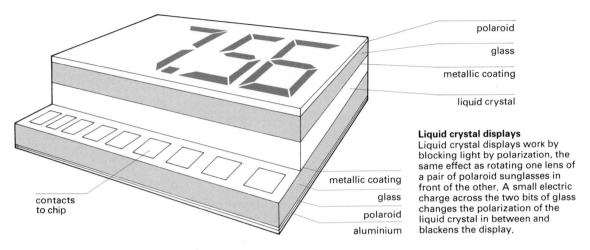

polaroid
glass
metallic coating
liquid crystal

metallic coating
glass
polaroid
aluminium

contacts to chip

Liquid crystal displays
Liquid crystal displays work by blocking light by polarization, the same effect as rotating one lens of a pair of polaroid sunglasses in front of the other. A small electric charge across the two bits of glass changes the polarization of the liquid crystal in between and blackens the display.

1 A liquid crystal display (LCD) works like sunglasses.
   An LCD blocks light by polarization.

2 An LCD is a thin film of liquid.
   It reacts to electrical charges.

3 It is placed in a glass sandwich.
   The sandwich has a top layer of plain glass and a bottom layer of reflective glass.

4 Transparent electrical conductors separate the crystals into segments.
   The segments form each digit.

5 Any digit can be formed.
   Up to seven segments are used.

6 The crystals are charged.
   Their molecules are arranged in one way.

7 The crystals are not charged.
   Their molecules are arranged in another way.

8 The conductors carry no charge.
   Light is reflected out again.
   The display is blank.

9 The conductors are charged.
   The molecules in the charged segments twist.
   They block light from the reflective surface.
   They appear black.

10 The charged surfaces appear as figures.

Task 10

Now divide your completed statements into two paragraphs:

Paragraph 1 will describe what an LCD is.
Paragraph 2 will explain how it works.

Give your text a suitable title.

25 Field engineer

Listening

John is 24 and a recent graduate. He's just been appointed as a trainee field engineer with an American oil services company.

The interview is in three parts:

1 The job
2 Qualifications and training
3 Work placement

Part 1 The job

Task 1

Before you listen, try to guess what kind of work a field engineer with an oil services company might do, and where he or she might work.

Task 2

As you listen, answer these questions:

1 How long has John had this job?
   a a few months
   b three months
   c two months
   d six months

2 What does he have to find out about when an oil company is drilling?
    a the rock
    b the oil
    c the sea
    d the drill

3 What kind of data do the sensors provide?
    a the depth of the hole
    b the resistivity of the rock
    c the quantity of oil
    d the hardness of the rock

4 Where has he been working most recently?
    a on-shore (on land)
    b on an oil tanker
    c off-shore (at sea)
    d in a laboratory

5 What is a 'dog house'?
    a a laboratory
    b a computer
    c a winch
    d a workshop

Task 3 Listen again and try to answer these questions:

1 What use can the oil company make of the data he provides?
2 How are the electronic sensors put in position?
3 What does he enjoy about the work?
4 Why does he have to work under pressure?
5 How is his operation totally 'self-contained'?
6 What do you think telemetry means?

Part 2 Qualifications and training

Task 4 As you listen, answer these questions:

1 What degree does he have?
    a a Master's in Electronics
    b a Bachelor's in Electronics
    c a Master's in Electrical Engineering
    d a Master's in Electronics and Electrical Engineering

2 How many trainees did the company appoint?
    a ten
    b eight
    c eighty
    d eighteen

3 What does the company provide for all trainees?
    a training for a degree
    b work placements
    c a three-month course
    d off-shore work

4 What did he like most about his study?
    a his work placement
    b being in Glasgow
    c working flat out
    d getting a holiday job in Germany

Part 3 Work placement

26 Telecommunications

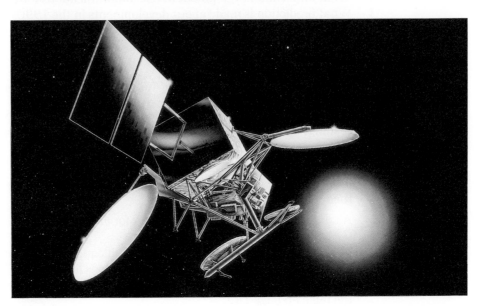

Tuning-in

Task 1

Put these developments in telecommunications in the order in which they were invented. Compare your answer with your partner.

a telex
b communication satellites
c modems
d telegraphy
e television

Now check your answers with Fig. 1 below.

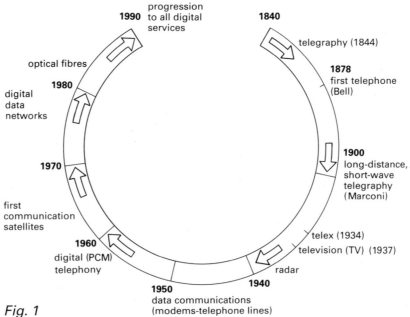

Fig. 1

Answer these questions with the help of Fig. 1.

1 Who invented the telephone?
2 What important development in telecommunications took place in the 1960s?
3 What prediction is made about developments in the 1990s?
4 When was telex introduced?
5 What form of telecommunications uses PCM?

Reading *Reading and note-taking*

Taking notes is a good way of remembering the important points in your reading, for either your study or work. When you take notes, you must:

1 identify the main points
2 record them in note form
3 organize your notes so that you can understand them easily when you read them again

A table is one way of organizing notes for easy access.

Task 3

Take brief notes from the text on the significance of the developments in telecommunications during one of the periods listed below. Your teacher will tell you which period to read about. Write your notes in the correct section of the table on page 142.

1 Nineteenth century
2 1901–1945
3 1946–1980
4 1980s on

Telecommunications: a brief historical review

para

The first true telecommunications system using electrical signals to carry messages started in the 1840s with machine telegraphy. Samuel Morse first developed the telegraph in 1832 but it was not until the mid-1840s that the system was put into practical use – sending coded electrical messages (Morse Code) along the wires. The telegraph became a rapid success, its speed quickly outdating the Pony Express for long-distance communications.   1

The next major step forward came in 1878 with the invention of the telephone by Bell. This enabled speech to be transported as electrical signals along wires and revolutionized personal communications.   2

In 1886, Hertz verified experimentally that electrical energy could be radiated and thus proved the existence of electromagnetic waves. This opened the way for the free-space transmission of information without wires. This provided the basis for all radio and TV broadcasting.   3

In 1901, Marconi established long-distance telegraph communication by transmitting between England and Canada. Although he did not realize it at the time, he achieved such long distances by reflecting radio waves in the ionosphere (layers of ionized gases and electrons existing in the earth's upper atmosphere at heights of 50–500 km). This overcame the problem of transmitting round the earth from one side of the Atlantic to the other.   4

25 With the discoveries of the diode and thermionic valve in the early 5
part of this century, advances were made in both receiver and
transmitter design with an associated impact in telegraphy,
telephony, and civil and military communications. Radio
broadcasting soon followed, with powerful transmitters serving to
30 communicate over wide areas. Television (TV) was first established
in 1937. Radar (radio detection and ranging) was also developed
from the 1930s and played a vital role in aircraft detection and
navigation in World War II.

As further advances in technology took place (e.g. the invention of 6
35 the transistor in 1947 and the subsequent development of
microelectronic integrated circuit technology), new applications
became feasible, and new systems were developed.

Data communications – the transmission of coded data (e.g. text, 7
graphics, financial information) between 'intelligent' terminals and
40 computers – was first established in the early 1950s using modems,
equipment which enables the telephone network to convey data as
well as speech. Other improvements in materials and devices also
led to the transmission of information via cables. Much of today's
long-distance telephone traffic is by submarine cable.

45 The space race led to yet another means of long-distance 8
communication, via fixed and mobile earth stations to satellites.
Today, several hundred satellites orbit the earth, and satellite links
provide all forms of communication and related services such as
telephony, data, TV, navigation, meteorology, and surveillance.

50 One of the very latest developments is the optical fibre cable – a tiny 9
glass fibre which can be used to convey signal information by light
pulses. Optical fibre cable with extremely low loss at low cost has
now been developed with very high data-carrying capacity. Several
thousands of telephone messages can be carried down a single
55 fibre.

Perhaps the greatest change which has occurred in the last twenty 10
years is that from analogue to digital methods of information
transmission. The very first commercially employed
telecommunication system, telegraphy, was and still is a digital
60 system. However, telephony, radio, and TV all started as analogue
systems. Today, the general trend is strongly towards the digital,
and within the next ten years the vast majority of
telecommunications systems will be digital. Problems of noise and
interference can be combated much more successfully in a digital
65 system.

The advances in microelectronics and the merging of 11
communications with computers have led naturally to the digital
transmission mode with its advantages of computer control,
automatic error checking of signals, excellent memory storage
70 facilities for data, and intelligent terminals. The market need for
vast quantities of information transmission and processing at very
high speed can only be reliably catered for by using digital
techniques. In fact the most rapidly growing field is almost certainly
in data communications employing high-speed digital techniques.

141

Development	Significance
Nineteenth century	
telegraphy (Morse)	_____
telephone (Bell)	_____
existence of electromagnetic waves proved (Hertz)	_____
1901–1945	
long-distance telegraphy via ionosphere	_____
valves	_____
radar	_____
1946–1980	
transistor	_____
data communications	_____
communications satellites	_____
1980s on	
optical fibre cable	_____
change to digital systems	_____
digital transmission mode	_____

Task 4

Exchange information with the others in your group to complete all sections of the table. Check with the text if there are any points you do not understand.

Language study *Simple Past* versus *Present Perfect*

Look at paragraph 1 of the text on page 140. Which tense is used most often? Why?

Now look through the text for examples of the Present Perfect. In which paragraphs do you find them? Why is this tense used here?

Study these sentences.

1 *Engineers **developed** optical fibre cables in the 1980s.*
2 *Optical fibre cables **have improved** the telephone system immensely.*
3 *Morse first **developed** the telegraph, a digital system, in 1832.*
4 *Digital systems of information transmission **have replaced** analogue systems in the last 20 years.*

Why is the Simple Past used in 1 and 3 and the Present Perfect in 2 and 4?

We use the Simple Past for events which took place in the past and are complete. Sometimes a day, date or time is given, e.g. *in 1832, on Tuesday.*

We use the Present Perfect for past events which have present results. This tense links the past with the present. Sometimes we use expressions such as *in the last twenty years, since the war, now* to show the link. Using the Present Perfect shows that we think the past events are of current relevance.

Task 5

Put each verb in brackets in the correct tense and form.

Alexander Graham Bell [1]_____ (invent) the telephone in 1878. He [2]_____ (be) a Canadian whose family [3]_____ (come) from Scotland. Since then, telephone systems [4]_____ (grow) dramatically; in the UK alone there [5]_____ (be) now over 24 million lines. Formerly, the UK system [6]_____ (be) analogue. Many changes [7]_____ (take place) in recent years. Almost the entire UK network [8]_____ (be) now digital. Fibre optic cables [9]_____ (replace) the old copper lines. Previously, telephone exchanges [10]_____ (use) banks of electromagnetic relays for switching. Today, they [11]_____ (have) computer-controlled units. The new network [12]_____ (be) fast and reliable, allowing users access to many other communications services.

Task 6

Study these diagrams of old and new phones. Make a list of any differences. Compare your list with your partner.

carbon microphone

rotary dial

telephone line

older type telephone using rotor dialling, which generates pulses to code digits defining destination

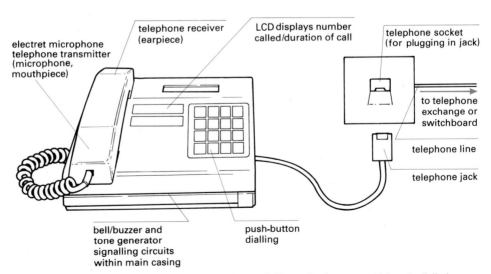

telephone receiver (earpiece)

LCD displays number called/duration of call

telephone socket (for plugging in jack)

electret microphone telephone transmitter (microphone, mouthpiece)

to telephone exchange or switchboard

telephone line

telephone jack

bell/buzzer and tone generator signalling circuits within main casing

push-button dialling

typical push-button type telephone (faster dialling using buttons, which code dialled digits into voice frequency tones to signal destination number).

In this description of the changes which have taken place in telephone design, put each verb in brackets in the correct tense and form.

Many changes [1]_____ (take place) in telephone design in recent years. Formerly, telephones [2]_____ (have) rotary dials. A pulse [3]_____ (signal) each dialled number. Now, push-buttons [4]_____ (replace) dials. Each button [5]_____ (trigger) a different audio-frequency tone. This [6]_____ (know) as multi-frequency dialling.

Also, the handset [7]_____ (change). Old models [8]_____ (contain) carbon microphones, which [9]_____ (be) inexpensive and robust but noisy. Today, moving-coil and electret devices [10]_____ (replace) the old microphones.

Advances in technology [11]_____ (allow) additional features to be added to phones. Most now [12]_____ (contain) memories to store frequently-used numbers. Some telephone manufacturers [13]_____ (add) LCDs which [14]_____ (display) dialled numbers and [15]_____ (indicate) the duration of calls.

Technical reading *Transmission lines*

Write down any types of cable and transmission lines used in telecommunications that you can think of.

Now read the text to find answers to the following:

1 Why are wires sometimes twisted together in transmission lines?
2 What is the purpose of the dielectric material in coaxial cable?
3 What frequencies can be carried by the following types of transmission lines?
   a coax
   b waveguides
4 What are the advantages of optical fibre cable?

Transmission lines

Telecommunications involves the transmission of information, including voice, data, TV, and radio over long distances. The transmission medium can be free space (ground, space, and sky waves), or the information can be guided between transmitters and
5 receivers using transmission line cables of various kinds. These include:

Parallel wires

This is the simplest type of transmission line consisting of a pair of insulated copper wires running side-by-side and covered by a plastic sheath (see Fig. 1). It is prone to interference and is only used to carry
10 information over small distances such as telephone connections within a building.

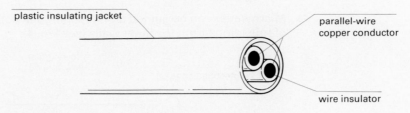

Fig. 1

Twisted pair

Two insulated copper wires are twisted together to reduce
interference effects and are enclosed in an insulating polyethylene
sheath (see Fig. 2). Because the wires are twisted, unwanted stray
15 signals picked up by one tend to be cancelled by similar signals picked
up by the other. They are used for communications over longer
distances, for example to connect telephones to their local exchange.

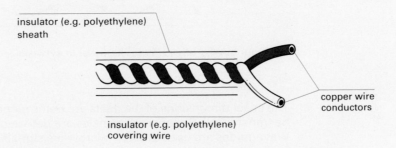

Fig. 2

Coaxial cable (coax)

Flexible coax has a copper wire core surrounded by copper braid. The
core and braid are insulated from each other by a dielectric material
20 such as polyethylene and covered by a PVC sheath (see Fig. 3).

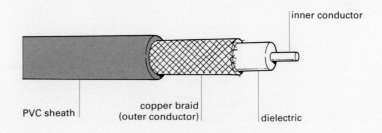

Fig. 3

The braid helps to screen the signals from interference. Coax can carry
a large number of signals over long distances at frequencies up to
1 000MHz. It is used to connect telephone exchanges and for cable
television.

Waveguides

25 Microwaves can be guided along rectangular copper ducts by a series of reflections from the inner walls (see Fig. 4).

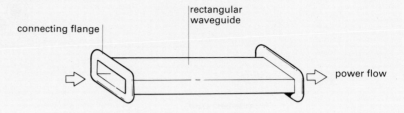

(a) rectangular waveguide for microwave transmission

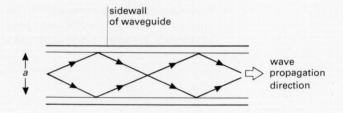

(b) 'guiding' of electromagnetic waves in a waveguide

Fig. 4

The exact dimensions of the ducts are determined by the frequency to be transmitted. Suitable frequencies are between 1GHz and 300GHz. Waveguides are used to carry microwave signals between dish aerials 30 and receivers.

Optical fibres

An inner core made from very pure silica fibre is surrounded by a similar glass sheath, known as cladding. This is covered by a protective plastic sheath. Non-visible light from lasers or LEDs can travel along the fibre by reflection from the surface where the core and 35 cladding meet (see Fig. 5).

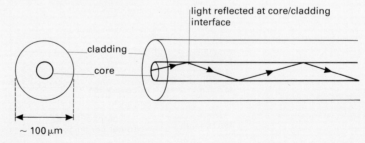

Fig. 5

Although the optical fibre has a smaller diameter than a human hair, it can be used to transmit tens of thousands of signals at high speed with very low loss and no interference from other signals. Optical fibre cable can be used in corrosive environments and is light, flexible and 40 cheap. This type of cable is gradually replacing conventional copper wire for connecting telephones and computer networks.

Task 9

Complete this table using information from the text.

Transmission line	Component materials	Examples of use
_____	_____	telephone connections within buildings
twisted pair	copper wire, plastic insulation	_____
_____	copper wire, copper braid, polyethylene sheath	trunk telephone lines, cable television
_____	copper ducts	_____
optical fibres	_____	_____

Task 10

Using information from the text on transmission lines and from Unit 10, note the transmission medium which could be used for each of the numbered links on this diagram.

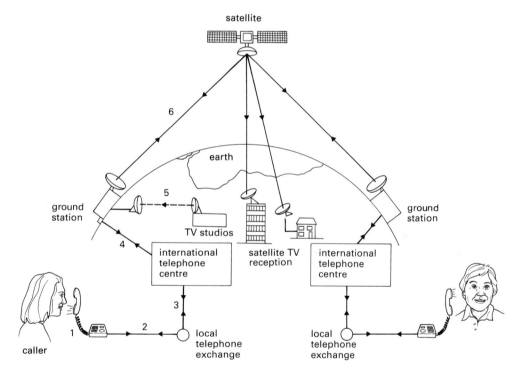

27 Cellphones

Tuning-in

Study this diagram of a cellphone. Note the buttons marked:

a SND   **c** PWR   **e** CLR   **g** FCN
b END   **d** STO   **f** PCL

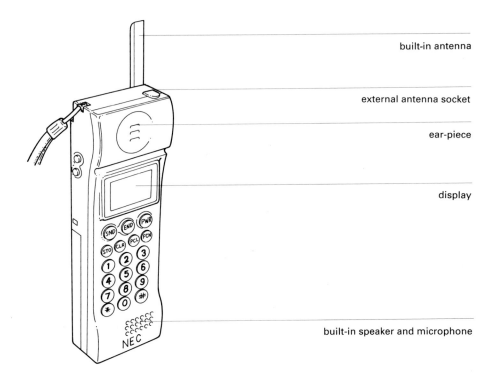

built-in antenna

external antenna socket

ear-piece

display

built-in speaker and microphone

Which buttons would you press for these operations? Justify your answers.

1 switching on or off
2 using one of the programming functions
3 deleting mistakes or individual numbers
4 finishing your call
5 starting your call after keying in the number

Task 2 Check your answers to Task 1 by reading quickly through this text.

Making a call

- Press PWR to turn the P3 on.

To prevent the phone being turned on or off accidentally, you need to hold down the PWR key to operate it.

- Key in the number.

- Press SND.

If you make a mistake when keying in a number and you want to delete the last digit:

- Press CLR briefly.

If you hold down CLR, the whole number will be deleted and the P3 will go back to standby.

You can dial a number of up to 32 digits, although only the last sixteen will be shown on the display at any time. To look at the first part of a number longer than sixteen digits:

- Hold down FCN.

When you have finished the call:

- Press END.

Reading   *Recognizing topic, locating detail*

When you are reading to find specific details, it is helpful if you can first identify the part of the text most likely to contain the details you want. If you can identify the best area to search, you have a better chance of finding the details quickly.

Task 3 Glance quickly through the text on the following page to identify which paragraph deals with the following:

a cellphone networks
b how signal levels are controlled
c how the MSC locates a cellphone
d limitations of mobile phone systems
e frequency distribution within cells and clusters
f the development of mobile phones
g how cellphones link with other cellphones and with the telephone system

Task 4

Decide which paragraphs are most likely to contain answers to these questions. Compare your decisions with your partner, then search for the answers.

1 Who uses mobile phones?
2 What does the MSC register of cellphones contain?
3 What is the difference between a mobile phone and a cellphone?
4 Why is a cellphone called a cellphone?
5 How large is a cell?
6 How does the MSC prevent interference due to too strong a signal level?
7 What's the best number of cells to form a cluster?
8 When were radiophones developed?
9 How does an MSC ensure that a cellphone is using the right frequency for a call?
10 What is the MSC permanently connected to?

Cellphones

para

Radiophones, using the VHF band, were developed during the Second World War to provide communications for ships and aeroplanes. At the end of the war they were further developed as mobile phones for use by the emergency services and other
5 services such as taxis.

1

With mobile phone systems, all communications take place through a central control base station. Mobile units normally do not communicate directly with other mobile units. They send messages to the control base station and the base station controller relays the
10 messages to other mobile units. Although mobile phones can be moved, they must stay within fixed areas. This type of system is limited by the fact that there are not enough VHF frequencies available for large numbers of communications between individual users.

2

15 The problem of a lack of suitable frequencies can be overcome by using a cellphone network. A cellular phone (cellphone) is a lightweight, portable radio transceiver which can transmit and receive telephone calls anywhere in the cellular network area. In the network, the same frequencies can be used for many different
20 telephone calls at the same time. To achieve this, each communications area is divided into a number of hexagonal-shaped cells, as shown in Fig. 1.

3

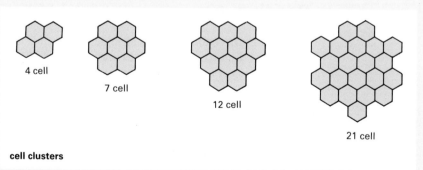

4 cell

7 cell

12 cell

21 cell

cell clusters

Fig. 1

para

4

Each cell is allocated a number of frequency channels for communications. Although the frequencies used in any one cell are
25 not used in its neighbouring cells, the same frequencies can be used in cells further away without causing interference. The size of the cells vary between 1 km to about 30 km across, depending on the output power of the cellphone transmitters. Each area can have a different number of cells, but a cluster of seven cells gives a good
30 compromise between the number of frequency channels available in each cell and the interference between communications in different cells.

5

Each cell has a small electronic base station situated in a public place such as a car park or shopping centre. All the base stations for
35 a cluster of cells are permanently connected to a main switching centre (MSC). This contains a computer to select suitable frequencies and control the communications for that cluster of cells. The MSC is also connected to other MSCs and to the public telephone exchange, allowing cellphones to make calls or receive
40 calls from other cellphones and fixed telephones throughout the whole telephone system (see Fig. 2).

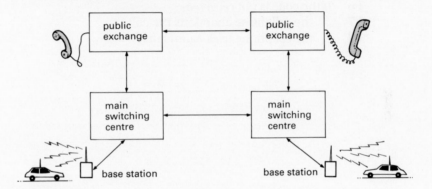

mobile and fixed networks

Fig. 2

6

The MSC keeps a register of cellphones indicating their cell position. If the cellphone moves to another cell, its new position is signalled to the MSC. In this way, the MSC knows where to send
45 signals to contact each cellphone. When a call is made to a cellphone, the MSC first checks the registrations to find the position of the cellphone. It then pages the cellphone and causes it to tune to the allocated frequency channel. The cellphone then begins sending an 8kHz signal to the base station. When the user takes the
50 call, the 8kHz signal is discontinued and the speech channel is enabled.

7

The base station constantly monitors the signal level of a call. If the signal level becomes too strong it will cause interference to other users. To prevent this, the power level of the cellphone is
55 automatically reduced. If the signal level becomes too weak, the MSC tests the signal strength from neighbouring base stations and switches the call to another base station and speech channel if necessary. This may cause a period of silence of up to about 400 ms while the switching takes place.

Writing *Linking facts and ideas, 6*

Task 5

Study these statements about making a cellphone call. Link them into longer sentences. You may omit words and make whatever changes you think are necessary in the word order and punctuation of the sentences.

1 A call is made from a cellphone.
2 The cellphone scans the available frequencies.
3 The cellphone finds the strongest signal to the nearest base station.
4 The cellphone detects that the base station is idle.
5 The cellphone transmits the required dialling code.
6 If the code is received, . . .
7 . . . the base station sends a signal back to the cellphone.
8 The signal indicates a suitable frequency channel for the call.
9 The cellphone tunes to the allocated channel.
10 The cellphone user hears the ringing tone.
11 The call is answered.
12 The user can speak and listen using the cellphone, as with a normal telephone.
13 The call is finished.
14 The cellphone signals to the base station.
15 The cellphone sends a short burst of signal at 8 kHz.
16 If the code is not received, . . .
17 . . . the cellphone abandons the call.
18 . . . the cellphone tries again later.

28 Data transmission

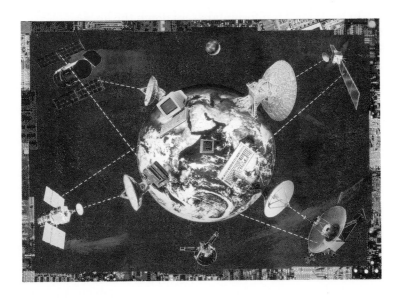

Tuning-in

Task 1

Study this diagram, which shows how a document can be sent from one fax machine to another.

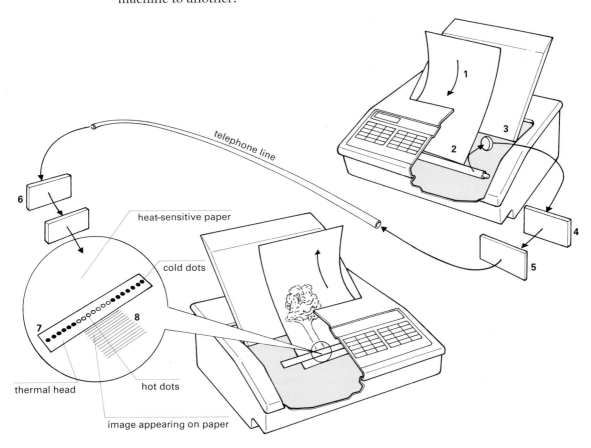

Now try to answer these questions.

1 How are fax machines linked?
2 How is the image transferred from the document to a microprocessor within the fax?
3 In what form is information sent down the lines?
4 In what form is information fed to the thermal head in the receiving fax?
5 How does the thermal head create images on paper?

Task 2

Read Text 1 to check your answers to Task 1 and to find the answers to any questions you were unable to answer from the diagram.

Text 1

1 A document is fed into the fax machine, face down.

2 It passes over a fluorescent tube which bounces light off the paper, reflecting the image on to a lens.

3 The lens passes the light on to a microprocessor which breaks the image down to a series of horizontal lines (7.7 lines to a millimetre).

4 Another microprocessor converts each line to a series of black and white dots, which are then coded, usually as '0' for black and '1' for white (binary code). This is in turn converted into digital information.

5 A third microprocessor (or modem) converts this information into signals, called analogue tones, which can be sent down telephone lines.

6 At the receiving machine, the analogue tones are converted back into binary signals and fed into a thermal head.

7 The thermal head is a mechanism containing a line of dots which heat up or cool down (in blocks of eight) depending on the electrical current supplied to them by the binary code.

8 The chemically treated paper reacts to heat along this line by forming black dots. As it passes across the thermal head, an image is formed corresponding to the information supplied by the binary code.

Reading *Comparing sources*

When trying to understand a difficult explanation, it is often useful to look at more than one source. There are a number of reasons for this:

1 Some sources are easier to understand than others.
2 By combining information from several sources, we can obtain a more complete explanation.
3 By reading about the same topic described in different ways, we can improve our understanding of written English and widen our vocabulary.

In this example, we are interested in how fax machines operate.

Task 3

Work in groups, **A** and **B**.

Group A: Compare Text 1 on page 154 and Text 2 below. Underline any points which help you to understand how a fax operates which are *only* found in Text 1. Compare your answers within your group.

Group B: Compare Text 1 on page 154 and Text 2 below. Underline any points which help you to understand how a fax operates which are *only* found in Text 2. Compare your answers within your group.

Text 2

FAX

para

Facsimile machines only came into widespread use in the late 1970s when international standards were set by the Comité Consultatif International Télégraphique et Téléphonique (CCITT), a body based in France. Before this, machines could only
5 communicate with those made by the same manufacturer.   1

Since then, facsimile technology has become increasingly sophisticated. The latest machines, which must be linked to a special digital phone line, can send a document to several places at once for the price of one phone call.   2

10 Facsimile transmission involves sending a document along a telephone line and converting the received signals into a reproduction of the original. 'Fax' machines can now send an A4 document, containing images as well as words, in less than a minute.   3

15 When you feed a document into the machine, a fluorescent lamp reflects the image on to a series of mirrors which reduce its size so that the whole document can be reflected on to a camera lens. The lens can only read the image in black and white. This information is converted, via a microprocessor, into binary information. The
20 machine records black as 0 and white as 1.   4

Another microprocessor then converts the binary data into digital information, which allows more data to be stored on the microchip. But, because most telephone systems cannot read digital information, this is again changed, via another microprocessor
25 (modem), into analogue tones, or pitches of noise. The first machine transmits these tones to the second.   5

The receiving machine converts the analogue tones back into digital and then binary information. It sends a signal (in binary code) to the thermal head, or printer. This turns heated elements on
30 or off according to the pattern of 0s and 1s contained in the signal. The pattern of black and white is then printed on to heat-sensitive paper.   6

Fax machines send information at the rate of 9,600 baud, or bits of information per second. A few seconds' interference on the phone
35 line can make several lines of a document illegible. If the line is noisy, the sending machine will slow down to reduce the amount of information lost.   7

Task 4   Which lines in Text 2 contain similar information to the paragraphs in Text 1?

Text 1 paragraphs	Text 2 lines
1	_____
2	_____
3	_____
4	_____
5	_____
6	_____
7	_____
8	_____

Task 5   Work in pairs. Discuss which text contains the best explanation. Which is the easier to understand?

Task 6   Find the references in Text 2 for each of the following:

1 a *body* based in France (lines 3–4)
2 *those* made by the same manufacturer (line 5)
3 The latest *machines* (line 7)
4 *This information* is converted (lines 18–19)
5 converts the *binary data* into digital information (lines 21–22)
6 The first machine transmits *these tones* (lines 25–26)
7 *It* sends a signal (in binary code) (lines 28–29)
8 If *the line* is noisy (lines 35–36)

Language study   *Reduced relative clauses*

One way of adding extra information to an explanation, or any other text, is to use relative clauses. For example:

1   *The thermal head is a mechanism.*
2   *The head contains a line of dots.*
1+2   *The thermal head is a mechanism* **which contains a line of dots**.

We can make this sentence shorter by omitting *which* and using an *-ing* clause:

   The thermal head is a mechanism **containing a line of dots**.

Study this example:

1   *The microprocessor converts the information into signals.*
2   *The signals are called analogue tones.*
3   *The signals are suitable for telephone transmission.*
1+2+3   *The microprocessor converts the information into signals,* **which are called analogue tones, which are suitable for telephone transmission**.

We can make this sentence shorter by omitting *which + to be*:

   The microprocessor converts the information into signals, **called analogue tones, suitable for telephone transmission**.

Task 7

Shorten this summary of the technical reading passage in Unit 26, pages 144–6, by reducing the relative clauses where possible.

> ### Transmission lines
>
> The lines which connect telephones within a building are the simplest type of transmission line, which consists of parallel wires. Those which link telephones to a local exchange may be twisted pairs, although these are being replaced. Coaxial cable, which is formed
> 5 from a copper core which is surrounded by a copper braid, is used to carry a large number of signals over long distances. The cables which provide connections between telephone exchanges are often coaxial. Waveguides, which are made of copper, are used to carry microwave signals between dish aerials and receivers. They are suitable for
> 10 frequencies which are between 1GHz and 300GHz. Optical fibres, which are made from very pure silica fibre, are the form of transmission line which is most often used these days.

Word study *Short forms*

Some technical words have common short forms. In some cases the short form is used much more frequently than the full form. For example:

Full form | Short form
a facsimile message | *a fax*

Task 8

What are the short forms for these terms?

1 amplifier
2 video recorder
3 television
4 potentiometer
5 coaxial cable

Task 9

What terms are represented by these short forms?

1 puff
2 phones
3 mike
4 CRT
5 phone

Writing *Describing transmission processes*

Task 10

Look at the flowcharts on the following page.

Study Flowchart 1, which describes in note form what happens when a document is fed into a fax machine.

Complete Flowchart 2 to describe how the data is received by the receiving machine. Use the diagram on page 153 and Texts 1 and 2 (pages 154 and 155) to help you.

Flowchart 1
Sending

Flowchart 2
Receiving

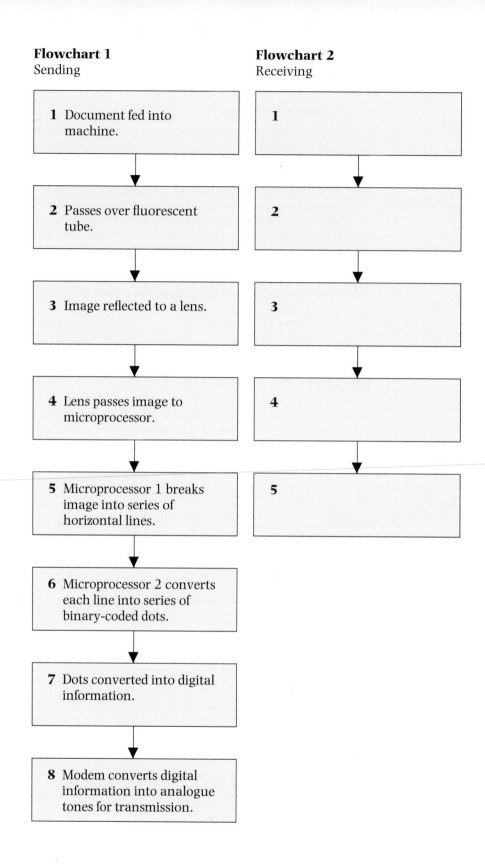

1 Document fed into machine.	**1**
2 Passes over fluorescent tube.	**2**
3 Image reflected to a lens.	**3**
4 Lens passes image to microprocessor.	**4**
5 Microprocessor 1 breaks image into series of horizontal lines.	**5**
6 Microprocessor 2 converts each line into series of binary-coded dots.	
7 Dots converted into digital information.	
8 Modem converts digital information into analogue tones for transmission.	

Task 11   Use the information contained in both flowcharts to write your own
description of how documents are sent by fax.

Technical reading *Communication services*

Read the text and then match these services with the given types of signal.

Communications service	**Type of signal transmitted**
1 telephone	**a** high-quality text, graphics characters
2 teletex	**b** video, speech
3 viewdata	**c** simple text, punctuation
4 radiopaging	**d** messages
5 fax	**e** radio signal, beep
6 videophone	**f** text, graphics, photographic images
7 e-mail	**g** speech
8 teletext	**h** interactive information, e.g. travel, shopping, banking
9 telex	**i** general information, e.g. news, sports results

Communications services

Telephones, connected by a network of cables, are commonly used for the two-way transmission of speech. The signals are switched from one line to another at switching centres known as telephone exchanges. Lines in a small area are switched by local exchanges,
5 local exchanges are connected through trunk exchanges, and trunk exchanges are connected to other countries by international exchanges. Such a system is called a Public Switching Telephone Network (PSTN) (see Fig. 1).

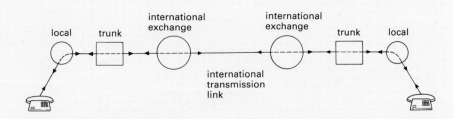

Fig. 1

Modern digital telephone networks can use videophones to transmit
10 video images as well as speech. The telephone network is used by video-conferencing services to interconnect small television studios. In this way, business people can hold conferences at a distance.

Public telephone networks are used by many other data communications services. One of the oldest is the telex system. This
15 enables messages, typed on teletype terminals, to be automatically printed by distant teleprinters. Telex can only transmit simple text containing capital letters and punctuation marks. It is also slow – about 100 words per minute (see Fig. 2).

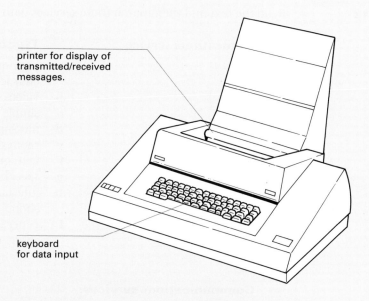

printer for display of
transmitted/received
messages.

keyboard
for data input

Fig. 2   Example of a teleprinter or teletype terminal

A newer, more advanced telex system, known as teletex, is also
20   available. This uses VDU terminals to transmit a variety of text and
graphics characters. High quality formats can be used and it is much
faster than telex, operating at speeds up to 2,600 words per minute
(see Fig. 3).

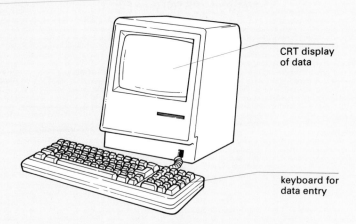

CRT display
of data

keyboard for
data entry

Fig. 3   A typical VDU-type data terminal

A facsimile (FAX) system allows the transmission of text, graphics and
25   photographic images.

Contacting people on the move is possible using a radiopaging
service. By carrying a small radio receiver called a radiopager, people
can be contacted wherever they are. Keying their number in on a
telephone causes the pager to beep. The person then goes to the
30   nearest telephone to get in touch with the caller.

A telephone network can be used to connect personal computers to an
electronic mail (e-mail) system. Messages sent from a personal

160

computer are stored on a central computer. Users can read and reply to these messages using their own computer.

35 Videotex or viewdata systems transmit pages of text and graphics through the PSTN to be displayed on a viewdata terminal or television screen. The data comes from a central computer. It is an interactive system, allowing the user to send messages back to the computer using a keyboard. The user can perform various tasks from home such
40 as ordering goods and controlling bank accounts.

A similar data communications service, known as teletext, uses the television broadcasting system rather than the PSTN. Text and graphics are transmitted as part of the television video signal. The user can switch between pages on the screen using special keys on a
45 remote control unit. Unlike viewdata, teletext is not interactive but does provide a similarly wide variety of useful information, such as news and travel information. Fig. 4 shows a teletext screen.

Fig. 4

An Integrated Services Digital Network (ISDN) is gradually being developed which uses telephone networks with microwave links and
50 satellite communications to interconnect all types of data communications services throughout the world.

Task 13   Which type of communications service would best meet these needs?

1   A travelling salesman whose office needs to contact him from time to time.
2   A company which wishes to hold a nationwide sales conference without bringing all its sales people to their headquarters.
3   Scientists in different universities who want to exchange ideas about their research.
4   A company which wishes to monitor and control its bank accounts without having to go to the bank every day.
5   Someone who wants instant access to sports results.
6   A reporter who wants to send a story to her newspaper from a remote location.
7   A police officer who wants to send a picture of a suspect as fast as possible to a police station at a distance.

29 Careers in electronics

Tuning-in

Task 1

List the areas of employment that you know of in electronics, for example, *Broadcasting*. List the types of jobs which are available in these areas, for example, *Maintenance*.

Task 2

Fill in the gaps in this text. Each gap represents one word. Compare your answers with your partner. More than one answer is possible for many of the gaps.

Careers in electronics

We are now [1]_____ the midst of the technological revolution which started [2]_____ the introduction of the microchip in the 1970s. More and [3]_____ electronic goods are being sold, especially computers, radio telephones, and leisure products. At the [4]_____ time, new applications

for electronics are ^{5}——————— found. Most domestic appliances now
^{6}——————— some form of electronic control. Petrol ^{7}——————— the filling
station and cash at the bank ^{8}——————— dispensed by electronic means.
Electronically-controlled pumps measure out drugs ^{9}——————— the
chronically ill. Electronic ignition and fuel management ^{10}———————
standard on cars.

All of this means ^{11}——————— career opportunities in electronics are growing.
More engineers are ^{12}——————— to design, plan, manufacture and install.
Service engineers are particularly ^{13}——————— demand although for the most
part they now replace panels ^{14}——————— than individual components. For
today's college and university graduates in electronics, ^{15}———————future is
bright.

Reading *Reading and sharing information*

The text which follows gives information on seven areas of employment. Read
the sections your teacher selects for you. Then explain to the others in your
group the career opportunities in those fields.

Using the information from the text and your own knowledge, discuss in your
group the advantages and disadvantages of each field of employment.

Areas of Employment

1 Avionics

Aircraft electronic equipment has to be maintained to a very high
standard with rigorous checks at set intervals. Service engineers are
required to maintain on-board equipment such as radio, radar, and
automatic flight path plotting equipment. Air traffic control equipment
5 is maintained on the ground.

2 Computing

This is an area where competition between companies is considerable
and technology is moving very quickly. With the increasing numbers
of computers used in the office, the home, and as part of industrial and
communications equipment, there is a growing need for engineers to
10 design these as well as service them. On the software side, there is
always a demand for programmers to design software for business
use and for leisure.

Almost every large business organization, like banks and insurance
companies, runs several local area networks (LANs). These require
15 network managers and maintenance and software support.

3 Defence

The reduction in political tension in recent years has meant cuts in the
defence industry. Nevertheless, many countries are still developing

sophisticated defence systems both for home use and for export.
These systems require not only engineers to design them, but highly-
20 skilled operators to man them and maintain them. Thus the armed
services recruit and train numbers of electronics technicians and
engineers.The major fields of defence electronics are:

1 early warning systems, e.g. radar
2 detection systems
25 3 ranging, using radar and computers
4 weapons guidance, using computers
5 communications

4 Industrial electronics

Industrial electronics started with transducers which allowed remote
monitoring of processes, especially those which involved high
30 temperatures or dangerous substances. Further developments
allowed processes in a whole range of industries – from food and
drink production to garbage recycling – to be fully automated.

The development of robotics has led to widespread application in the
car industry in particular. Everything from assembling to spraying the
35 completed car can now be done without human assistance. Tedious
and unpleasant jobs have disappeared. Automation has led to savings
for the manufacturer but has also contributed to unemployment.
Electronics engineers are required to design and service industrial
circuits, including control panels.

5 Leisure products

40 Society expects a wide range of leisure electronic items. This can be
gauged by sales of radio, hi-fi equipment, television sets, compact
disc players, video recorders, satellite receivers, etc. Engineers and
technicians are required not only to design and manufacture these,
but also to maintain them.

6 Telecommunications and broadcasting

45 People today expect to be able to get in touch with each other at any
time and in any place. The communication of speech, text, and other
data by cable and radio is a growing field of employment. Cellphones
are an area of recent expansion.

Engineers are employed to manufacture, plan, install, commission,
50 and maintain telecommunication equipment. National and local radio
and television stations employ broadcasting and sound engineers.

7 Medical equipment

Recent years have seen a sharp increase in equipment for patient care.
This ranges from body scanners to electronic stethoscopes. While the
operation of this equipment is the responsibility of the medical team,
55 engineers are required to work with medical experts in the design of
such equipment, in the installation of larger equipment, and in
maintenance. Job satisfaction in this area can be high.

Speaking practice

Task 4

Work in pairs, **A** and **B**. Note any advantages and disadvantages for each type of employment using information from your partner and from your texts. You may add any opinions of your own.

Student A: Your texts are on page 180.
Student B: Your texts are on page 187.

Type of employment	Advantages	Disadvantages
Manufacturing		
Planning		
Installation		
Commissioning		
Maintenance		
Sales		
Teaching		
Research & Development		

Word study   *Topic sets, 2*

Task 5

Group these technical terms into the topic sets below.

base station   flicker   microprocessor
cell   flyback   program
counter   LCD   quartz
data   logic gate   raster
divider   MSC   scan

Topic sets:

1   digital watch
2   cellphones
3   computers
4   television display

Writing   *Describing career plans*

Task 6

Write a brief description of your career plans, using information of your own and from this unit.

30 Job ads

Wanted Engineering Staff

Communicate, a go-ahead company involved in the design, development, and production of VHF/UHF communications equipment and accessories, are looking for engineers for the following jobs:

Trainee Service Engineers (two posts)

Applicants should either have practical knowledge in RF communications or have qualifications in the field of electronics with/without practical knowledge.
Salary: Negotiable, depending on experience.

Service Engineer

Applicant should have at least two years' experience in servicing VHF/UHF communications equipment down to component level. The successful applicant will be servicing land-mobile, marine, and amateur radio products.
Salary: According to experience.

Analogue RF Design/Development Engineer

Applicants should have an HNC or BSc in Electronics or Telecommunications and should have experience in RF product design with an understanding of mechanical assembly.
Salary: According to qualifications and experience.

CVs for the attention of: Mr Clark
Head of Personnel
Communicate (UK) Limited
Tradescant House
Lewis Avenue
LONDON NW3 1BR

Reading   *Understanding job ads*

Task 1

Study the job advertisement above. Answer these questions:

1 What is the name of the company?
2 What are its activities?
3 Where is the company based?
4 How many posts are vacant?
5 Which posts are available to those without experience?
6 How do you apply for a post?
7 Who is Mr Clark?
8 What salaries are offered?

Task 2

Charles Dunkin decides to apply for one of the Trainee Service Engineer posts. Look at his CV below and his letter of application on the following page.

Imagine you are Mr Clark of Communicate (UK) Limited. List Charles' strong points and his weak points.

Applicant   *Charles Dunkin*

Strong points   _____

     _____

Weak points   _____

     _____

CURRICULUM VITAE

Personal details	Name: Charles Dunkin Date of birth: 30 May 1974 Address: 44 Maxton Street, Bath, BL14 6FH Marital status: Single

Education
1991–present
	Maxwell College of Further Education, Bath
	Ordinary National Certificate in Electronics
	I will complete my ONC studies in June. I have already successfully completed modules in:
	    Digital Electronics 1 & 2
	    Analogue Electronics 1 & 2
	    CAD
	    Computing
	    Mathematics
	    Communication Skills

1985–1990	Bath Secondary School
	General Certificate of Education
	    Physics A
	    Mathematics B
	    English B
	    Geography C
	    French C

Other qualifications	Clean driving licence.
Work experience Summer 1992	Service technician, Baird Audio-Visual Products, Bath This vacation job gave me experience of servicing domestic television sets, VCRs, and radios
1990–1991	Trainee Mechanic, Dunkin's Garage, Bath
Summer 1989	Waiter, Western Hotel, Bath
Hobbies/interests	Motorcyle maintenance Football-College 2nd XI

Referees	**Academic**
	Dr John Coulter
	Head of Department of Electronics
	Maxwell College of Further Education
	BATH BW4 6BN **Work**
	     Ms Jean Çadmus
	     Head of Personnel
	     Baird Audio-Visual Products
	     Farrer Lane
	     BATH BL41 3LH

```
                                              44 Maxton Street
                                              Bath
                                              BL14 6FH

          Mr Clark
          Head of Personnel
          Communicate (UK) Limited
          Tradescant House
          Lewis Avenue
          LONDON
          NW3 1BR

          3 April 19__ __

          Dear Mr Clark

          Re: Trainee Service Engineers

          I would like to apply for the post of Trainee Service
          Engineer, as advertised in the April issue of Electronics
          Today. I enclose my CV with the names of two referees.

          I consider I am well qualified for this post. I will shortly
          complete my ONC in Electronics and will be available for
          employment from the end of June. My college work has been good,
          and I have completed all my modules successfully to date.

          On leaving school, I worked for one year in the family garage.
          Although I decided not to continue with this career, it gave
          me useful work experience. Last summer I spent two months of my
          vacation working for a small company which repairs electronic
          equipment. This provided valuable experience in servicing
          television sets, radios, and VCRs. I feel confident that my
          work experience, together with my college qualification, make
          me well suited for the post.

          I have a clean driving licence and enjoy good health.

          I look forward to hearing from you.

          Yours sincerely

          Charles Dunkin

          Charles Dunkin
```

Listening

Task 3

Study Fig. 1. It shows the organizational structure of Communicate (UK) Ltd. Try to guess some of the functions of the different departments.

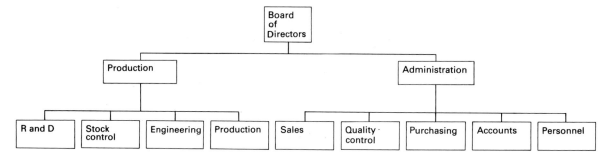

Fig. 1

Task 4 🔲 Mr Clark of Communicate (UK) Ltd, briefs a new trainee. Work in pairs, **A** and **B**.

Listen to the tape and find out the function of these departments:

Student A	**Student B**
Production	Engineering
Stock control	R and D
Sales	Quality control
Purchasing	Accounts
Personnel	

Note your findings in the table below. When you have completed your section of the table, share your findings with your partner so that you can both complete the table.

Functions of departments in Communicate (UK) Ltd.

Production	**Administration**
Production	Sales
Engineering	Quality control
Stock control	Purchasing
R and D	Accounts
	Personnel

Speaking practice

Task 5

Discuss in your group what you should and should not do when invited for interview by a company. Write out your advice in note form like this:

You should:	You should not:
1	1
2	2
3	3
4	4
etc.	etc.

Task 6

Exchange your notes with another group. Compare their advice with yours.

Task 7

This table lists the commonest cause of failure at interviews, as reported by four UK companies employing electronics graduates. How many of the problems listed did your group identify?

Company	Commonest cause of failure at interview
AB Electronic Products Group	Lack of awareness of how AB operates. Inability to communicate in straightforward non-jargon language.
Mars Group	Lack of preparation. Interviewees are often unaware of the range of qualities required and react badly to unexpected general questions which have not been properly considered beforehand.
NE Technology Ltd	Inability of applicants to apply their academic knowledge to practical problems. Subjects studied are understood only in theoretical terms. Applicants are often unable to express themselves effectively to demonstrate their particular abilities, perhaps because of lack of preparation.
Rolls Royce plc	Candidates are inadequately prepared – not only in their knowledge of the work and products of Rolls Royce plc, but in their own attributes and experience.

Task 8

1   Work in pairs, **A** and **B**.

Student A: Play the part of Mr Clark. Write five questions to ask Charles Dunkin at his interview.

Student B: Play the part of Charles. Write five questions you think Mr Clark might ask you at your interview. Prepare suitable answers.

2   Conduct the interview.

Task 9

Study the job advertisements on the following pages and try to find suitable jobs for these candidates:

1   A technician with experience in servicing hospital equipment.
2   An engineer who would like to work in broadcasting.
3   Someone who wants a job which provides a car.
4   Someone who wants a job with a lot of travelling.
5   An engineer who wants to work in the USA.
6   Someone who wants to work in developing countries and who does not require a large salary.

7 A technician with experience in servicing all kinds of communications equipment.
8 An electronics engineer who wants to work in Europe and who speaks English, Italian, and German.

Compare your choice with your partners.

a

Trainee Location Engineers

This company has two vacancies for people to train as Location Engineers working on Broadcast and Corporate programmes. Successful applicants would be joining one of America's foremost suppliers of location video crews. Once trained, they can look forward to interesting work which includes travel both in the USA and abroad.

Applicants should have a suitable qualification in Electronics, Telecommunications, or similar. A clean driving license and preferably some practical experience of domestic VHS machines and televisions would be an advantage.

Please supply contact telephone number with application in writing to:

Joan Berridge
General Manager
Sunset Film & Video Limited
4900 University Avenue
SAN DIEGO
California
USA

b

Electronic Engineers

Extremely competitive salaries.
If you would like to hear about outstanding opportunities in Europe to work in the expanding area of personal communication systems, write to:

Euroengineer Ltd
Austin Street
Norwich
NJ2 1BL
Enclose your CV and the names of two referees. Applicants should have a degree or equivalent in electronics or a related discipline. A good command of foreign languages woud be an advantage.

c

Wanted urgently
Practical people for the Third World

We seek practical people with skills to pass on to the developing world. You can help to link up the developed and the developing world.

If you can fill one of these vacancies, contact us at once.

Current requests include:

☐ **Studio Electronics Engineer**

☐ **Refrigeration/Radio/ TV Engineers**

☐ **Hospital Electronics Engineers**

☐ **Electrical Engineers for instruction/ installation**

☐ **Electronics Instructors**

☐ **Lecturers in Power and Communication**

☐ **Maintenance and Repair Technician**

For more details, please write to:
LINK, 10 Summer Gardens, London, SW14 2LH.

Conditions of work:
- Pay based on local rates
- Posts are for a minimum of 2 years
- You should be without dependants
- Many employers will grant leave of absence

I'm interested. I have the following training/ experience:

_____

Name _____

Address _____

LINK
Linking the developed and developing worlds

---

d

Angel Recruitment

Radiocomm Systems
Repair and service RF and VHF communications equipment.
Salary negotiable+car
London

Medical Equipment
Maintain and fault-find x-ray and scanning equipment.
Salary negotiable +car
South Coast

Data-Processing Support
Provide technical support on disk drives throughout Europe.
Salary negotiable.
Geneva

Paging Systems
Service and repair of pocket pagers. Travel within Birmingham and surrounding area.
Salary negotiable+car
Birmingham

Microprocessor Systems
Complex fault-finding of digital and micro systems. Extensive travel in UK and overseas.
Salary negotiable.
Essex

Write to: Karen Crawley, BSc. Angel Recruitment, Winchester Hampshire SO19 1QB

Task 10   Complete your CV.

CURRICULUM VITAE

Personal details

Name   _____

Date of birth   _____

Address   _____

                        _____

                        _____

Marital status   _____

Education   _____

                        _____

                        _____

Work experience   _____

                        _____

                        _____

Hobbies and interests _____

                        _____

Referees

Academic   Work

_____   _____

_____   _____

_____   _____

Task 11   Write a letter of application for one of the jobs advertised in this unit. Base your letter on the one shown in Task 2 on page 168.

Student A
Speaking practice

Unit 1

Task 10

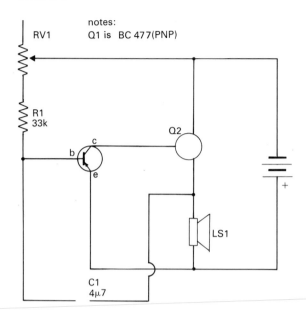

notes:
Q1 is BC 477(PNP)

RV1

R1
33k

b
c
e
Q2

LS1

C1
4μ7

+

Unit 5

Task 7

Cell	Mercury	Lithium
Type	?	primary
Output voltage	1.35V	?
Applications	? hearing aids, watches, calculators	backup for computer RAM memories, ?
Usual size	?	button and small cylindrical cells
Advantages	small size but high energy	? high voltages, last for long periods at low currents
Disadvantages	?	lithium is poisonous, used cells should be disposed of carefully

Unit 8

Task 5

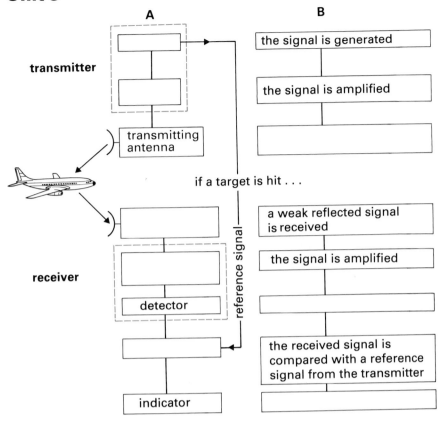

A   B

transmitter

| the signal is generated |

| the signal is amplified |

transmitting antenna

if a target is hit . . .

reference signal

receiver

| a weak reflected signal is received |

| the signal is amplified |

detector

| the received signal is compared with a reference signal from the transmitter |

indicator

Unit 9

Task 7

Find out from your partner how to:

1   measure the current in this circuit.
2   check a fuse.

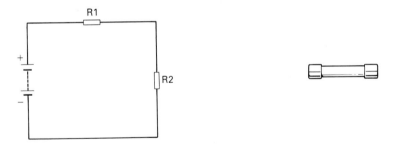

This information should help you to advise on your partner's problems.

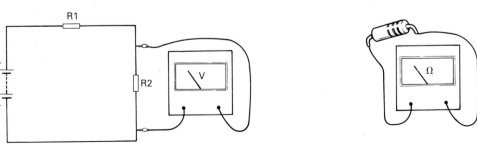

Unit 10

Task 6

Frequency band	Some uses
Very low (VLF) 3kHz–30kHz	?
Low (LF) ?	long-wave radio and communication over large distances
Medium (MF) 300kHz–3MHz	?
? (HF) 3MHz–30MHz	short-wave radio and communication, ?
Very high (VHF) 30MHz–300MHz	FM radio, police, meteorology devices
? (UHF) 300MHz–3GHz	TV (bands 4 and 5) and aircraft-landing systems
Super high (SHF) (microwaves) ?	radar, communication satellites, ?

Unit 13

Task 6

Find out from your partner the missing values in these amplifier specifications. Ask him or her to explain items 4–7.

Provide the information your partner requires. Explain with the help of the passage below what items 1–3 mean. Your partner also has Figs. 1 and 2.

1	voltage gain	40dB
2	frequency response	20Hz to 20kHz at −3dB
3	distortion	less than 0.1% THD
4	S/N ratio	?
5	input impedance	?
6	output impedance	?
7	supply voltage	?

Amplifiers

Amplifiers are used in almost all electronic circuits. In audio systems, the very small signal voltages produced by microphones, tape recording heads, magnetic pickup heads, etc. are amplified by a pre-amp. A power amp is then used to enable the signals to drive a
5   loudspeaker.

The gain of an amplifier is measured by comparing its output with its input. If a logarithmic scale is used, the gain is expressed in decibels (dB). In a pre-amp we are interested in the voltage gain, but in a power amp the power gain is more significant.

10   The gain of an amplifier is almost constant over a range of input signal frequencies. However, because of capacitance effects, the gain falls by 3dB at the upper and lower cut-off frequencies, as shown in Fig. 1.

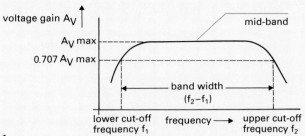

voltage gain A_V

A_V max

$0.707\ A_V$ max

mid-band

band width
$(f_2 - f_1)$

lower cut-off
frequency f_1

frequency →

upper cut-off
frequency f_2

Fig. 1

The useful frequency response of an amplifier is the range of
frequencies between these two −3dB cut-off points. The size of this
15 range is known as the band width.

Ideally, the output signal will be an enlarged copy of the input signal.
However, when the input signal level becomes too high, an amplifier
no longer behaves in a linear fashion and distortion of the output
signal occurs (see Fig. 2). This normally occurs when the output
20 voltage is greater than half the supply voltage.

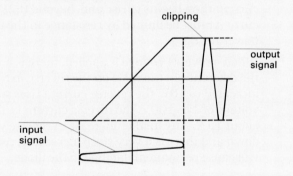

clipping

output
signal

input
signal

Fig. 2

Such clipping of the output signal causes the generation of a number
of unwanted harmonic waves in the amplifier. The overall effect of this
phenomenon for the whole amplifier is known as the total harmonic
distortion (THD). The percentage THD is obtained by comparing this
25 distortion with the maximum amplifier output.

Unit 16

Task 6

The Digital Compact Cassette (DCC) (1992) was developed by Philips. Like
ordinary audio cassettes, this system uses magnetic tape but packaged in more
robust form like a mini CD box. Unlike ordinary cassettes, digital recording is
used with the result that the sound quality is as good as CDs – much better
than ordinary audiotape. A major advantage over CDs is that the DCC can be
re-recorded.

An attraction of DCCs is 'backwards compatibility'. This means that you can
play conventional audio cassettes in the same machine as DCCs. There is no
need then to throw away your cassette library. With a double-deck machine,
you can re-record your cassettes in digital form. DCCs have several hours
recording capacity.

Unit 18

Task 7

Describe this graph in sufficient detail for your partner to sketch it. If you have problems, the text which follows may help you

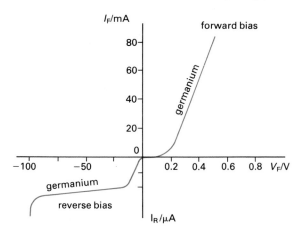

As a forward bias is applied to a germanium diode, the forward current remains negligible until a voltage of about 0.15V is reached. The forward current then begins to rise and, beyond 0.2V, it rises steeply. The forward current must be limited by resistance in the circuit to keep the diode within its power rating.

When a reverse voltage is applied, there is a very small reverse current (note the difference in the scale on the reverse axes). As the reverse voltage is increased to 10V, the reverse current rises steadily to 2μA. Between a reverse voltage of 10−100V, the reverse current is almost constant, only rising by about 1μA. Any further increase in reverse voltage causes the diode to break down and there is a very steep increase in reverse current. If not prevented, this will cause permanent damage to the diode.

Use this matrix to help you sketch your partner's graph.

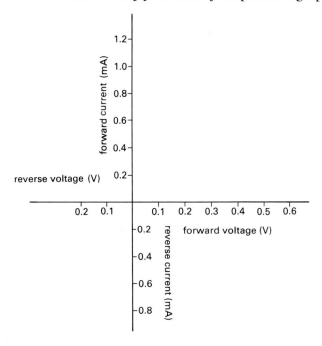

Unit 21

Symptom	Cause	Remedy
Power doesn't turn on.	Mains lead is not connected.	Connect mains lead to the mains outlet.
	?	?
Power is on but unit doesn't operate.	Safety devices are operating.	Turn off On/Off switch and disconnect mains cord. Then reconnect and switch on again.
TV programmes cannot be recorded.	?	?
Timer recording doesn't work.	?	?
	Timer Record Function is set to OFF.	Set Timer Record Function to ON.
	?	?
	Clock is flashing 0:00.	Set clock time and perform timer setting.
Playback picture is not in colour.	?	?
Playback picture has large amounts of 'snow'.	TV set is not properly tuned to the video playback channel of the VCR.	Retune TV set.
	Video heads are clogged with dirt.	?
	?	Use new tape.

Unit 29

1 Manufacturing

Manufacturing includes making anything from individual components or printed circuit boards to complete pieces of equipment such as televisions. In the case of the latter, it is usual to break down the equipment into modules and manufacture these separately. For
5 instance, television sets are manufactured in this way with each set consisting of up to seven individual modules. When the modules come off the assembly line, they are passed to groups of testers and troubleshooters to check for faults. The various modules are then assembled to produce the complete unit. The disadvantage of this
10 kind of work is the monotony and the time pressure of assembly line work.

2 Planning

Firms with large communications networks require planners. For instance, telecommunications network providers need to know where to place exchanges for maximum switching capability, and microwave
15 towers for minimum interference. They also need to know the sizes of cables to handle traffic growth.

Rapidly springing up everywhere from a number of different suppliers are the radio mobile, cellular, and paging networks. All these require careful planning and field surveys to prevent mutual interference. Job
20 opportunities will grow in this sector.

3 Installation

There is a wide range of installation work required, for example, installing exchanges, LANs, and medical equipment. Such work involves cabling and may require some knowledge of mechanical engineering if special racks and even entire rooms have to be
25 constructed to accommodate equipment. Installation work usually involves travel which can be overseas depending on the product involved.

4 Commissioning

Once equipment is installed, it needs to be commissioned, i.e. put into operation. Problems often emerge at this stage which have to be
30 ironed out. This work is usually done by engineers with long experience in the type of equipment being commissioned.

Student B
Speaking practice

Unit 1

Task 10

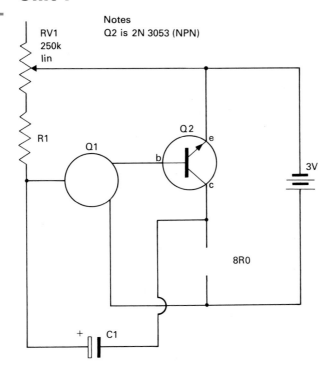

Notes
Q2 is 2N 3053 (NPN)

RV1
250k
lin

R1

Q1

Q2

b

e

c

3V

8R0

+ C1

Unit 5

Task 7

Cell	Mercury	Lithium
Type	primary	?
Output voltage	?	3V
Applications	cameras, hearing aids, watches, ?	? photographic equipment
Usual size	button	button and ?
Advantages	? but high energy	long storage life, high voltages, last for long periods at low currents
Disadvantages	expensive	? used cells should be disposed of carefully

Unit 8

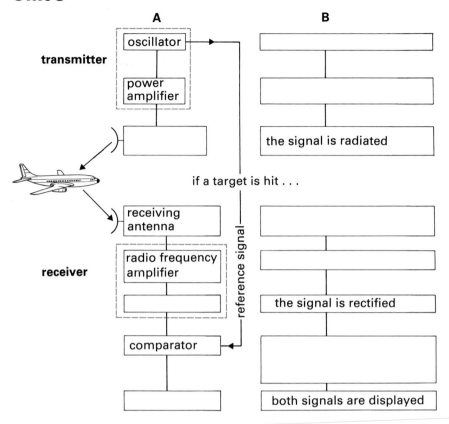

A   B

transmitter

oscillator

power amplifier

the signal is radiated

if a target is hit . . .

receiving antenna

receiver

radio frequency amplifier

reference signal

comparator

the signal is rectified

both signals are displayed

Unit 9

Task 7

Find out from your partner how to:

1   measure the voltage drop across R2 in this circuit.
2   check the value of this resistor.

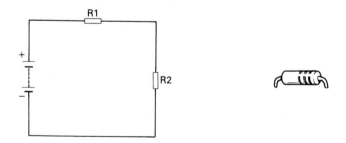

This information should help you to advise on your partner's problems.

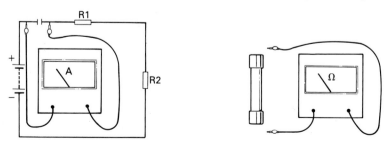

Unit 10

Frequency band	Some uses
Very low (VLF) ?	communication with submarines
Low (LF) 30kHz–300kHz	? and communication over large distances
? (MF) 300kHz–3MHz	medium wave, local and distant radio
High (HF) ?	short wave radio and communication, amateur and CB radio
Very high (VHF) 30MHz–?	? , police, meteorology devices
Ultra high (UHF) 300MHz–3GHz	TV (bands 4 and 5) and ?
? (SHF) (microwaves) above 3GHz	? , communication satellites, telephone and TV links

Unit 13

Task 6

Find out from your partner the missing values in these amplifier specifications. Ask him or her to explain items 1–3. Explain to your partner with the help of the passage below what items 4–7 mean. Your partner also has Figs. 1 and 2.

1	voltage gain	?
2	frequency response	?
3	distortion	?
4	S/N ratio	greater than 65dB
5	input impedance	50 kilohm
6	output impedance	600 ohm
7	supply voltage	+9V to +12V

Amplifiers

Amplifiers are used in almost all electronic circuits. In audio systems, the very small signal voltages produced by microphones, tape recording heads, magnetic pickup heads, etc. are amplified by a pre-amp. A power amp is then used to enable the signals to drive a
5 loudspeaker.

Any unwanted signals in an amplifier are known as noise. Unfortunately, noise is randomly produced inside most circuit components such as resistors, capacitors and semi-conductors. This type of noise is amplified and heard through the loudspeakers as hiss
10 and crackle. Noise is also induced by the low frequency mains supply. This may be heard through the loudspeaker as hum. The ratio of noise to signal power is known as the S/N (signal-to-noise) ratio and is

normally expressed in dB. For hi-fi sound reproduction, the S/N ratio must have a value greater than 70dB. Tape cassette recorders can only 15 achieve this S/N level by using special noise reduction systems such as Dolby or Dbx.

To prevent voltage and power loss, the input and output impedance of an amplifier must be matched to the other parts of the system. These impedances are measured in ohms. For minimum voltage loss, an 20 amplifier's input impedance should be high and its output impedance should be low.

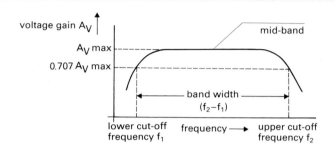

Fig. 1.

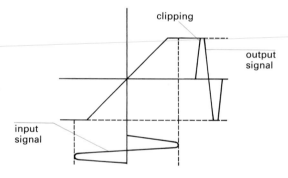

Fig. 2.

Unit 16

Task 6

One recent recording system is a magneto-optical system called the MiniDisc (MD) produced by Sony. It uses a combination of a laser and a magnetic field to read and write data on plastic discs almost half the size of a CD. One advantage of this system over digital tape is that it gives random access to individual tracks rather than serial access, i.e. it can immediately jump to any part of the recording rather than having to play from the beginning to the end.

In the MD system, as in CD systems, the sound is sampled at 41.1kHz but the data is compressed by 20% to give a 74-minute recording capacity. Because of the low power requirement of the laser, the system can be operated from a battery, making it compact and portable. It is also shock-proof. The MiniDisc can be re-recorded and, as with other digital systems, there is almost no quality loss when discs are copied.

Unit 18

Task 7

Describe this graph in sufficient detail for your partner to sketch it. If you have problems, the text which follows may help you.

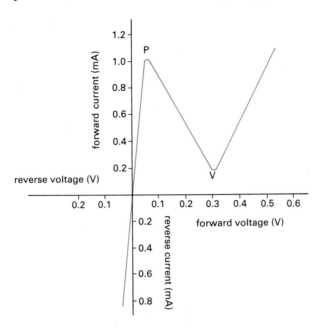

The graph shows the characteristics of a tunnel diode. As the forward voltage is increased, the current increases steeply until point P is reached. This is the peak point. The peak voltage for a germanium tunnel diode is about 0.05 volts. After P the current falls sharply until V. V is the valley point. From P to V the diode has a negative resistance. The forward voltage at V is about 0.3 volts. After the valley point, the current increases steadily with increased voltage and the diode behaves like a normal diode. When a reverse voltage is applied, however, the reverse current rises steeply, unlike other diodes.

Use this matrix to help you sketch your partner's graph.

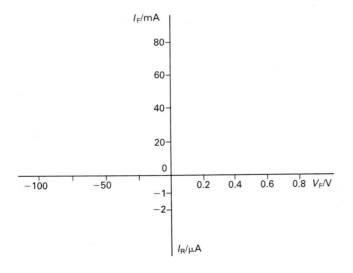

Unit 21

Symptom	Cause	Remedy
Power doesn't turn on.	?	?
	Timer is set to ON.	Set Timer to OFF.
Power is on but unit doesn't operate.	?	?
TV programmes cannot be recorded.	Aerial lead is not connected.	Connect aerial lead correctly.
Timer recording doesn't work.	Recording start or stop time setting is incorrect.	Set recording start and stop time correctly.
	?	?
	Clock shows incorrect time.	Adjust clock to present time.
	?	?
Playback picture is not in colour. Playback picture has large amounts of 'snow'.	Reception channel was not adjusted correctly during recording.	Readjust reception channel.
	?	?
	?	Consult qualified service personnel.
	Tape is old and/or defective.	?

Unit 29

5 Maintenance

As electronic equipment has become more complex, so maintenance technicians have become more specialized. For instance, technicians who used to service both radio and television may now specialize in either radio and audio equipment or television sets and video
5 recorders. Similarly, technicians now specialize in servicing computers, telecommunications equipment, medical equipment, industrial robots, and so on. Testing and fault-finding equipment has become more sophisticated. Oscilloscopes are commonplace on workbenches, and programmable analysers are available for carrying
10 out a full range of diagnostic tests on particular types of equipment. Although these save a great deal of time, they can make the work of the service technician less challenging. Service men and women are always in demand.

6 Sales

Sales staff too require specialist knowledge – not so much of how the
15 equipment works, but what it is capable of and the differences between similar types of equipment. They also have to know the advantages of their company's products over those of their rivals. Although selling ability is more important than technical expertise, it is not unusual for service technicians to transfer to sales.

20 Most salespeople work on a commission basis. In addition they usually have use of a company car. They can earn high salaries and are crucial to the success of a company. Selling usually involves a great deal of travel and can be stressful.

7 Teaching

Colleges and universities employ substantial numbers of graduates in
25 electronics. Colleges prefer teaching staff who also have experience in industry or business. Universities look for teaching staff with research experience. Salaries in education tend to be lower than in industry. Technicians are also employed in educational institutes in laboratories and workshops to assist with research and to provide maintenance.

8 Research and Development

30 Large companies run their own R & D departments. Exciting opportunities exist for creative engineers in the design and testing of new products. Such opportunities are limited. Most R & D work is carried out at the company's headquarters. Many electronic companies are multinationals, so the R & D work may not be done in the country where the product is assembled.

Appendix 1
Glossary of electronic terms and abbreviations

The definitions in this glossary refer to words only as they are used in this book. The meanings of certan words will vary according to context. As the texts in this book are authentic and come from a variety of sources some inconsistency in hyphenation and spelling is inevitable.

How to use the Glossary

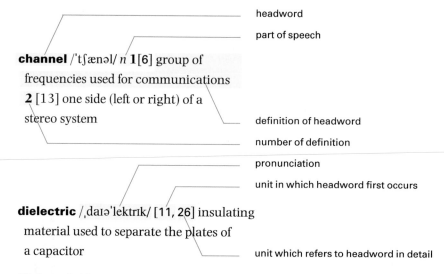

headword

part of speech

channel /'tʃænəl/ *n* **1** [6] group of frequencies used for communications **2** [13] one side (left or right) of a stereo system

definition of headword

number of definition

pronunciation

unit in which headword first occurs

dielectric /ˌdaɪə'lektrɪk/ [11, 26] insulating material used to separate the plates of a capacitor

unit which refers to headword in detail

Abbreviations used in the text

n = noun
v = verb
adj = adjective

absorber /əb'sɔːbə(r)/ [10] device which takes in energy
absorption /əb'sɔːpʃn/ [10] process of absorbing
AC /eɪ 'siː/ [5] alternating current
acoustics /ə'kuːstɪks/ [7] measure of how well sounds can be heard
adaptor /ə'dæptə(r)/ [22] device for changing one type of socket into another type of socket
ADC /ˌeɪ diː 'siː/ [15] analogue-to-digital converter
A/D converter /eɪ 'diː kən,vɜːtə(r)/ analogue-to-digital converter

address bus /ə'dres bʌs/ [23] set of parallel conductors in a computer for carrying address signals from the CPU to the memory and I/O devices
Advanced Television /əd,vɑːnst 'teləvɪʒn/ [20] name for new American television system which provides clearer, more detailed, high quality images and very high quality sound
aerial /'eərɪəl/ [1] device for collecting or sending out signals being transmitted through free space
AF /ˌeɪ 'ef/ [1, 11] audio frequency
align /ə'laɪn/ [21] bring into line with

alternating current /ˈɔːltəneɪtɪŋ ˌkʌrənt/ [5] current which regularly changes direction backwards and forwards

aluminium /ˌæluˈmɪnjəm/ [5, 23] light metal (Al) used to make heatsinks

AM /ˌeɪ ˈem/ [10] amplitude-modulated

ammeter /ˈæmmiːtə(r)/ [15, 19] electronic instrument for measuring current

amp /æmp/ [1] *see* amplifier

amplification /ˌæmplɪfɪˈkeɪʃn/ [10] increase in the magnitude of voltage or power

amplifier /ˈæmplɪfaɪə(r)/ [1] electronic circuit for increasing the size of a signal

amplify /ˈæmplɪfaɪ/ [5] make bigger (e.g. voltage or power)

amplitude /ˈæmplɪtjuːd/ [10] size of a wave at any given time

amplitude-modulated /ˌæmplɪtjuːd ˈmɒdjʊleɪtɪd/ [1, 10] with the size of the carrier wave varied according to the changing size of the signal being carried

analog /ˈænəlɒg/ *see* analogue

analogue /ˈænəlɒg/ [3] able to take on any value between an upper and lower limit

analogue-to-digital converter /ˌænəlɒg tə ˌdɪdʒɪtl kənˈvɜːtə(r)/ [12] electronic circuit which changes analogue signals into digital signals

analogue tones /ˈænəlɒg təʊnz/ [28] audio signals produced by a modem for sending through telephone lines

AND gate /ˈænd geɪt/ [23] digital logic gate which only has a high output when all its inputs are high

anode /ˈænəʊd/ [19] positive electrode which attracts electrons

answerphone /ˈɑːnsəfəʊn/ [1] telephone with a built-in tape recorder to allow messages to be recorded

antenna /ænˈtenə/ [8] *see* aerial

Aquadag /ˈækwədæg/ [19] carbon compound used to prevent a voltage build-up on an oscilloscope screen

arithmetic and logic operations /əˌrɪθmətɪk ənd ˈlɒdʒɪk ɒpəˌreɪʃnz/ [23] mathematical processes carried out by the CPU in a computer

array /əˈreɪ/ [13] *see* matrix

assembly line /əˈsemblɪ laɪn/ [14] production area of a factory where the parts of a product are put together in a series of stages

astigmatism control /əˈstɪgmətɪzm kənˌtrəʊl/ [19] control to adjust the sharpness of focus of a beam making the spot in a cathode ray tube round rather than oval

attenuate /əˈtenjuːeɪt/ [10] reduce the magnitude of a signal

attenuator /əˈtenjuːeɪtə(r)/ [10] electronic circuit for reducing the magnitude of a signal

ATV /ˌeɪ tiː ˈviː/ [20] Advanced Television

audible /ˈɔːdɪbl/ [9] able to be heard

audio /ˈɔːdɪəʊ/ [1] to do with sound

audio amplifier /ˌɔːdɪəʊ ˈæmplɪfaɪə(r)/ [12] device for increasing the volume of sound signals

audio frequency /ˌɔːdɪəʊ ˈfriːkwənsɪ/ [10] sound signal frequency between 15Hz and 20kHz

audio-visual /ˌɔːdɪəʊ ˈvɪʒʊəl/ [30] to do with both sound and graphics

Autocad /ˈɔːtəʊkæd/ [2] name of a popular computer drawing and design program

avionics /ˌeɪvɪˈɒnɪks/ [29] application of electronics in aircraft

back EMF /ˈbæk iː em ˈef/ [9] voltage induced in an inductor in opposition to the original voltage

back-up /ˈbæk ʌp/ *n* [9] substitute kept in reserve for emergencies

balance control /ˈbæləns kənˌtrəʊl/ [13] control for adjusting the relative amplification of the left and right channels of a stereo signal

balance wheel /ˈbæləns wiəl/ [24] small wheel which controls the timing in a watch

band width /ˈbændwɪtθ/ [21] difference between the lowest and highest frequency in a group of frequencies

bargraph /ˈbaːgraːf/ [6] electronic meter which shows the power level of a signal using columns of lights (usually LEDs)

base /beɪs/ *n* [9] electrode of a transistor which is used to control the flow of charge carriers between the collector and the emitter

base station /ˈbeɪs ˌsteɪʃn/ [27] transmitter and receiver which controls all the mobile radio communications in a particular area

bass /beɪs/ [6] low frequency sounds

battery /ˈbætərɪ/ [1, 5] combination of cells for providing electrical energy

battery charger /ˈbætərɪ ˌtʃaːdʒə(r)/ [5] device for recharging a battery

baud /bɔːd/ [28] bits per second: measure of the rate of transmission of digital signals

beam /biːm/ [6, 8] narrow, straight path for electrons or radio waves

bias /ˈbaɪəs/ [5] apply a DC voltage to a component (e.g. a transistor) to control its operating point

binary /ˈbaɪnərɪ/ [3, 15] counting system using only two digits, 0 and 1

binary digit /ˈbaɪnərɪ ˌdɪdʒɪt/ [15] one character in a binary system, either 0 or 1

bipolar transistor /ˌbaɪpəʊlə trænˈzɪstə(r)/ [23] transistor containing two PN junctions forming either an NPN or a PNP type of transistor

bistable /ˌbaɪˈsteɪbl/ [24] electronic circuit which can be switched between two stable states

bit /bɪt/ [15] binary digit

blank /blæŋk/ *v* [20] make a video signal blacker than black

blank /blæŋk/ *adj* [24] not showing anything

block /blɒk/ [1] *see* stage

block diagram /ˌblɒk ˈdaɪəgræm/ [1] drawing showing the different electronic stages which make up a circuit

body scanner /ˈbɒdi ˌskænə(r)/ [29] medical electronic device for building up a video image of the internal organs of a patient

braid /breɪd/ [26, 28] conductor loosely woven from metal threads

bridge (circuit) /brɪdʒ (ˈsɜːkɪt)/ [18] balanced circuit made from four components

bridge rectifier /ˌbrɪdʒ ˈrektɪfaɪə(r)/ [5] circuit made up of four diodes for converting both the positive and negative parts of an AC voltage to DC

brightness /ˈbraɪtnəs/ [8, 19] strength of light

brilliance /ˈbrɪliəns/ [19] *see* brightness

broadcasting /ˈbrɔːdkɑːstɪŋ/ [29] transmitting radio or TV signals

broadcast quality /ˈbrɔːdkɑːst ˌkwɒləti/ [22] of a high enough standard to be used for a professional radio or TV broadcast

buffer /ˈbʌfə(r)/ [8] electronic circuit for isolating two circuits from each other and matching the signals going between them

burglar alarm /ˈbɜːglər əˌlɑːm/ [13] system for detecting when someone tries to break into a building and steal something

burst /bɜːst/ [27] sudden explosive pulse

bus /bʌs/ [23] set of parallel conductors for carrying signals between the various internal parts of a computer system

button /ˈbʌtn/ [8] small push switch (usually round)

buzzer /ˈbʌzə(r)/ [9] device which uses an electrical signal to produce a buzzing sound

C

cable /ˈkeɪbl/ [26, 29] insulated wire or set of wires used for carrying electrical current or signals

cable television /ˌkeɪbl ˈtelɪvɪʒn/ [26] system which transmits video signals using cables

cabling /ˈkeɪblɪŋ/ [27] insulated electrical wiring

CAD /kæd/ [2, 3] Computer Aided Design: technical drawing and design using a computer

cadmium /ˈkædmɪəm/ [5] chemical element (Cd) used in some batteries

calculator /ˈkælkjʊˌleɪtə(r)/ [8] electronic device for doing mathematical calculations

camcorder /ˈkæmˌkɔːdə(r)/ [21] portable hand-held camera for recording and playing video images

capacitance /kəˈpæsɪtəns/ [5] ability to store charge

capacitor /kəˈpæsɪtə(r)/ [1, 4] electronic component which stores charge

carrier wave /ˈkærɪə weɪv/ [1] radio wave used to carry audio or video signals

cathode /ˈkæθəʊd/ [19] negative electrode which emits electrons

cathode ray oscilloscope /ˈkæθəʊd reɪ ɒˌsɪləskəʊp/ [19] electronic instrument for measuring and displaying changing signals on a screen using a cathode ray tube

cathode ray tube /ˈkæθəʊd reɪ tjuːb/ [19] large thermionic valve used to produce a display by firing a beam of electrons at a phosphor-coated screen. Used in oscilloscopes and television sets

CB radio /ˌsiː biː ˈreɪdɪəʊ/ [10] amateur mobile radio system

CCITT /ˌsiː siː aɪ tiː ˈtiː/ [28] Comité Consultatif International Télégraphique et Téléphonique

CD /ˌsiː ˈdiː/ [1, 16] compact disc

cell /sel/ **1** [5] component which changes a form of energy (usually chemical) energy into electrical energy **2** [27] subdivision of a communications area in a cellular phone network. Each cell has its own base station and set of transmission frequencies

cellphone /ˈselfəʊn/ [15, 27] *see* cellular phone

cellular phone /ˌseljʊlə ˈfəʊn/ [27] mobile telephone which communicates through base stations situated in areas called cells

central processing unit /ˌsentrəl ˈprəʊsesɪŋ ˌjuːnɪt/ [23] IC chip at the centre of a computer for controlling the system and processing the data

ceramic /səˈræmɪk/ [4] material commonly used as an insulator

channel /ˈtʃænəl/ *v* [6] guide into channels

channel /ˈtʃænəl/ *n* **1** [6] group of frequencies used for communications **2** [13] one side (left or right) of a stereo system

characteristics /ˌkærəktəˈrɪstɪks/ [11] relationships between quantities which show how a component responds in different situations

charge /tʃɑːdʒ/ *v* [5] put an electrical charge into a component such as a battery or a capacitor

charge /tʃɑːdʒ/ *n* [19] basic property of electricity, either positive (+) or negative (−)

chip /tʃɪp/ [8] *see* microchip

chip count /ˈtʃɪp kaʊnt/ [23] number of IC chips used in a circuit

circuit /'sɜːkɪt/ [1] closed path around which a current can flow

circuit diagram /'sɜːkɪt 'daɪəgræm/ [1] drawing using standard symbols to show how electronic components are connected together

circuitry /'sɜːkətrɪ/ [12] collection of electronic circuits

cladding /'klædɪŋ/ [26] glass sheath surrounding the pure silica fibre core of an optical fibre cable

clipping /'klɪpɪŋ/ [13] distortion in which the tops of a signal are cut off

cluster /'klʌstə(r)/ [27] group of cells in a cellular telephone network

CMOS /'siːmɒs/ [23] complementary metal oxide semiconductor

coax /'kəʊæks/ [26] coaxial cable

coaxial /kəʊˈæksɪəl/ [28] made from two conductors with the same central axis

coaxial cable /kəʊˈæksɪəl ˌkeɪbl/ [26, 28] solid copper wire surrounded by copper braid which has very low losses when used for transmitting high frequency signals

coil /kɔɪl/ [10] spiral of wire used as an inductor

collector /kəˈlektə(r)/ [1] electrode of a transistor which collects charge carriers travelling from the emitter

combinational logic /ˌkɒmbɪˈneɪʃnəl ˈlɒdʒɪk/ [23] system which obeys mathematical rules of logic in which the output is dependent on the combination of the inputs

Comité Consultatif International Télégraphique et Téléphonique /ˌkɒmɪˈteɪ kɒnsuːlˈtæˈtiːf ˈanteənæsɪŋˈnæl telegræˈfiːk e telefɒˈniːk/ [28] committee based in France which sets standards for international communications

commission /kəˈmɪʃn/ v [29] bring a piece of equipment into operation

common-emitter configuration /ˌkɒmən ɪˈmɪtə kənfɪgəˌreɪʃn/ [11] connection of a transistor so that the emitter is part of both the input and the output circuit

compact disc /ˌkɒmpækt ˈdɪsk/ [1, 16] plastic disc used to store high quality sound recordings as a pattern of pits on its surface

comparator /kəmˈpærətə(r)/ [8] electronic circuit for comparing two signals

compilation /ˌkɒmpɪˈleɪʃn/ [7] collection of recordings grouped together

complementary configuration /ˌkɒmplɪmentrɪ kənfɪgəˈreɪʃn/ [11, 13] connection of a matched PNP and NPN transistor in a push-pull circuit

complementary metal oxide semiconductor /ˈkɒmplɪmentrɪ metl ɒksaɪd ˌsemikənˈdʌktə(r)/ [23] family of integrated circuits containing combinations of field effect transistors

complementary transistors /ˌkɒmplɪmentrɪ trænˈzɪstəz/ [13] matched pair of PNP and NPN transistors used in a push-pull configuration

component /kəmˈpəʊnənt/ [1] basic part of a circuit

compression /kəmˈpreʃn/ [7] amplification of weak audio signals and reduction of strong audio signals to limit the sound range

computer /kəmˈpjuːtə(r)/ [23] general purpose electronic device that uses a program to process data

computing /kəmˈpjuːtɪŋ/ [29] study and application of computers

conduct /kənˈdʌkt/ v [10] allow current to flow

conduction /kənˈdʌkʃn/ [10] process of conducting

conductive /kənˈdʌktɪv/ [6] allows current to flow

conductivity /ˌkɒndʌkˈtɪvətɪ/ [10] property of a material which indicates the ease with which a current can flow through it

conductor /kənˈdʌktə(r)/ [10] material which allows current to flow

cone /kəʊn/ [13] conical shaped stiff paper part of a loudspeaker which vibrates to produce sound waves

contact /ˈkɒntækt/ [13] connection point

contrast /ˈkɒntrɑːst/ n [8] difference between light and dark areas of a video image

control bus /kənˈtrəʊl bʌs/ [23] set of parallel conductors for carrying control signals from the CPU to the other parts of a computer system

control grid /kənˈtrəʊl grɪd/ [19] charged metal plate which uses varying voltages to control the number of electrons reaching the anode in a thermionic valve and the brightness of the display in a cathode ray tube

control panel /kənˈtrəʊl ˌpænl/ [29] unit which contains the circuits and knobs used for controlling and adjusting a machine

controller /kənˈtrəʊlə(r)/ [27] person who operates a mobile radio base station and controls the system

convert /kənˈvɜːt/ [12] change from one form into another

copper core /ˌkɒpə ˈkɔː(r)/ [26, 28] central solid conductor

counter /ˈkaʊntə(r)/ [24] electronic circuit for counting pulses

CPU /ˌsiː piː ˈjuː/ [23] central processing unit

crackle /ˈkrækl/ [13, 16] noise heard through loudspeakers which is randomly produced inside electronic components or caused by dust and static on the surface of a vinyl record

critical frequency /ˌkrɪtɪkl ˈfriːkwənsɪ/ [10] particular frequency at which there is a significant change in the response

CRO /ˌsiː ɑːr ˈəʊ/ cathode ray oscilloscope

crossover network /ˈkrɒsəʊvə ˌnetwɜːk/ [13] electronic circuit for dividing an audio signal into high, medium, and low frequencies and sending them to the appropriate loudspeaker

CRT /ˌsiː ɑː ˈtiː/ [18, 19] cathode ray tube

current /ˈkʌrənt/ [5] flow of electrons

current collector /ˈkʌrənt kəˌlektə(r)/ [5] the carbon rod in a zinc-carbon cell

cut-off frequency /ˈkʌt ɒf ˌfriːkwənsɪ/ [13] frequency at which the audio output of an amplifier falls by 3dB from the mid-range value

cycle /ˈsaɪkl/ [13] one complete part of the repeating pattern of a wave

D/A converter /ˌdiː ˈeɪ kənˌvɜːtə(r)/ digital-to-analogue converter

DAC /ˌdiː eɪ ˈsiː/ [15, 16] digital-to-analogue converter

data /ˈdeɪtə/ [18, 23] information to be processed

data bus /ˈdeɪtə bʌs/ [23] set of parallel conductors for carrying data signals between the various internal parts of a computer system

data comms /ˈdeɪtə kɒmz/ data communications

data communications /ˌdeɪtə kəmˌjuːnɪˈkeɪʃnz/ [26, 28] transmission of information by electronic means

dB /ˈdesɪbel/ [13] decibel

Dbx /ˌdiː biː ˈeks/ [13] audio noise reduction system

DC /ˌdiː ˈsiː/ [5] direct current

DCC /ˌdiː siː ˈsiː/ [16] digital compact cassette: digital magnetic tape cassette used for high quality reproduction of sound

de-energize /diːˈenədʒaɪz/ [9] remove the energy from

decibel /ˈdesɪbəl/ [13] tenth of a bel: logarithmic ratio for comparing power. Used to measure sound.

deck /dek/ [7] recording mechanism

decode /ˌdiːˈkəʊd/ [8] convert a digitally coded signal back to its original form

decoder /ˌdiːˈkəʊdə(r)/ [24] electronic circuit for converting digitally coded signals back to their original form

decouple /ˌdiːˈkʌpl/ [23] provide an escape path for unwanted signals

decoupling /ˌdiːˈkʌplɪŋ/ [8] process of shorting unwanted signals to earth

defective /dɪˈfektɪv/ [21] faulty

deflect /dɪˈflekt/ [10] cause to move away from a straight path

deflection /dɪˈflekʃn/ [19] movement away from a straight path

deflection system /dɪˈflekʃn ˌsɪstəm/ [19] metal coils or plates in a cathode ray tube which use varying voltages to change the direction of the electron beam and move it to different positions on the screen

demodulator /diːˈmɒdjʊleɪtə(r)/ [1] electronic circuit for separating a signal from its carrier wave

detect /dɪˈtekt/ [12] discover the presence of

detector /dɪˈtektə(r)/ [1] *see* demodulator

device /dɪˈvaɪs/ [9] piece of equipment which performs a particular function

diagnostic test /ˈdaɪəgnɒstɪk test/ [27] test to find out what is wrong with a piece of equipment

dialling code /ˈdaɪəlɪŋ kəʊd/ [27] coded telephone signal which is transmitted to establish contact with a particular telephone

diaphragm /ˈdaɪəfræm/ [24] thin plate which moves easily when a small amount of pressure is applied to it

dielectric /ˌdaɪəˈlektrɪk/ [11, 26] insulating material used to separate the plates of a capacitor

digit /ˈdɪdʒɪt/ [15] one character in a number system

digital /ˈdɪdʒɪtl/ [1, 2] having only discrete levels (usually two levels)

digital logic /ˌdɪdʒɪtl ˈlɒdʒɪk/ [19] electronic system in which the inputs and outputs can switch between two states (high and low) and always obey fixed mathematical rules of logic

digital-to-analogue converter /ˌdɪdʒɪtl tuː ˌænəlɒg kənˈvɜːtə(r)/ [15] electronic circuit for changing digital signals into anologue signals

diode /ˈdaɪəʊd/ [1, 4] semiconductor component which only allows current to flow in one direction

direct current /ˌdaɪrekt ˈkʌrənt/ [5] current which flows in one direction only

disc /dɪsk/ [1, 16] *see* compact disc

disk /dɪsk/ [6] thin flat circular component used to store data

disk drive /ˈdɪsk draɪv/ [30] computing device for reading and writing on magnetic disks

discharge /dɪsˈtʃɑːdʒ/ v [10, 23] remove or lose electric charge

discrete component /dɪˌskriːt kəmˈpəʊnənt/ [5] separate component rather than being part of an integrated circuit

dish aerial /ˈdɪʃ ˌeərɪəl/ [26, 28] hemispherical device used for collecting and sending out microwaves for transmission through free space

dissipate /ˈdɪsɪpeɪt/ [11] gradually release energy

distortion /dɪˈstɔːʃn/ [6, 7] unwanted change of shape of a signal

divider /dɪˈvaɪdə(r)/ [24] electronic circuit which reduces the frequency of a signal to a submultiple of the original frequency

dog house /ˈdɒg haʊs/ [25] a workshop on an off-shore drilling platform

Dolby /'dɒlbɪ/ [13] common audio noise reduction system

domestic appliance /də,mestɪk ə'plaɪəns/ [29] device used in the home

double-deck machine /'dʌbl dek mə'ʃiːn/ [16] two tape recorders combined in one unit and sharing a common amplifier

double-pole switch /,dʌbl 'pəʊl swɪtʃ/ [5] switch with two sets of contacts which can be used to connect and disconnect two circuits (or parts of a circuit) simultaneously

drive /draɪv/ [22] wheel, controlled by an electric motor, which forces the tape rollers in a tape recorder to turn and move the magnetic tape

drum kit /'drʌm kɪt/ [15] set of drums

drum machine /'drʌm mə,ʃiːn/ [15] electronic device for automatically producing drum sounds

duct /dʌkt/ [26] hollow rectangular tube

E

earpiece /'ɪəpiːs/ [26] part of a telephone which contains a small loudspeaker and is held against the user's ear

earth /ɜːθ/ n [1] common zero voltage point in a circuit

earth /ɜːθ/ v [1] connect to a zero voltage point

earth station /'ɜːθ ,steɪʃn/ [26] satellite communications transmitter/receiver base positioned on earth

electret microphone /ɪ,lektret 'maɪkrəfəʊn/ [26] capacitor microphone which contains a permanently charged insulating material known as electret

electricity /ɪlek'trɪsətɪ/ [5] supply of electric current and voltage

electrode /ɪ'lektrəʊd/ [5] positive or negative connector which collects or emits a charge

electrolyte /ɪ'lektrə,laɪt/ [5] chemical which aids the flow of current between electrodes

electrolytic capacitor /ɪ'lektrə,lɪtɪk kə'pæsɪtə(r)/ [1, 5] capacitor which uses an electrolyte to give large values of capacitance. It must be connected with the correct polarity.

electromagnetic field /ɪ,lektrəʊmæg,netɪk 'fiːld/ [12] area around a conductor in which electromagnetic force has an effect

electromagnetic induction /ɪ,lektrəʊmæg,netɪk ɪn'dʌkʃn/ [12] the production of a voltage caused by a changing electromagnetic field

electromagnetic wave /ɪ,lektrəʊmæg,netɪk 'weɪv/ [10] travelling wave which displays electrical and magnetic properties

electromagnetism /ɪ,lektrəʊ'mægnətɪzm/ [2] magnetism caused by an electric current

electron /ɪ'lektrɒn/ [18, 19] negatively charged particle

electron gun /ɪ'lektrɒn gʌn/ [18, 19] part of a cathode ray tube which accelerates electrons towards the display screen

electron lens /ɪ'lektrɒn lenz/ [19] part of a cathode ray tube which focuses the electrons into a narrow beam

electronic /elek'trɒnɪk/ adj [1] to do with electrons

electronic mail /,elektrɒnɪk 'meɪl/ [28] communications system which uses a central computer and computer terminals for the transmission of messages

electronics /elek'trɒnɪks/ n [2, 3] the science and technology of electrons and electronic devices

electronic engineer /'elek,trɒnɪk endʒɪ'nɪə(r)/ [29] person who is professionally qualified in the study of electronics

electroplating /ɪ,lektrəʊ'pleɪtɪŋ/ [6, 17] process using electricity to cause a chemical reaction which deposits a metallic surface on an object

electrostatic charge /ɪ'lektrəʊstætɪk 'tʃɑːdʒ/ see static

electrotechnology /ɪ,lektrəʊtek'nɒlədʒɪ/ [2] the technology of electrical systems

e-mail /'iː meɪl/ [28] electronic mail

EMF /,iː em 'ef/ [5] electromotive force: voltage produced by an electrical source (e.g. a battery)

emit /ɪ'mɪt/ [8] give out

emitter /ɪ'mɪtə(r)/ [12] electrode of a transistor which gives out charge carriers

energize /'enədʒaɪz/ [13] provide energy to

EQ /'iː 'kjuː/ [6] equalization

equalization /,iːkwəlɪ'zeɪʃn/ [6] amplification of different frequencies of a signal by different amounts

erase head /ɪ'reɪz hed/ [21] magnetic tape recorder head for removing the magnetically stored data from the tape

exchange /ɪks'tʃeɪndʒ/ [26] see telephone exchange

F

facsimile machine /fæk'sɪməliː mə,ʃiːn/ [28] electronic device for sending documents and graphic images over long distances

fader /'feɪdə(r)/ [6] electronic circuit which allows the volume of a sound recording or the brightness of a video recording to be gradually reduced

fax /fæks/ [28] **1** see facsimile machine **2** the document sent through a facsimile machine or the communications service which uses facsimile machines to transmit documents over long distances

feed reel /'fiːd riːl/ [21] video recorder reel which holds and gives out the magnetic tape before it passes the heads

ferrite (rod) core /ˌferaɪt (rɒd) 'kɔː(r)/ [10, 24] solid cylinder of metal oxide insulating material placed in the centre of a coil to concentrate the magnetic field

ferromagnetic /ˌferəʊmæg'netɪk/ [9] exhibiting the same magnetic behaviour as iron

FET /ˌef iː 'tiː/ [23] field effect transistor

field /fiːld/ [20] one half of a video frame

field effect transistor /ˌfiːld ɪ'fekt træn'zɪstə(r)/ [23] transistor in which N-type and P-type semiconductors are used to form a channel through which the current must flow. The current is controlled by voltages which change the width of the channel.

field engineer /ˌfiːld endʒɪ'nɪə(r)/ [25] engineer who works at the site of an installation rather than in an office or factory

field scan signal /'fiːld skæn ˌsɪgnəl/ [20] part of a video signal which controls the movement of the spot down a television screen

field sync pulse /'fiːld sɪŋk pʌls/ [20] part of a video signal which adjusts the timing for the display of a frame on a television screen

filament /'fɪləmənt/ [19] very thin wire which gives off heat or light when a current is passed through it. Used in lamps and as a heater element in thermionic valves.

filter /'fɪltə(r)/ [8] electronic circuit for removing unwanted signals

flicker /'flɪkə(r)/ [20] unsteadiness of a video picture

flip-flop /'flɪp flɒp/ [24] digital electronic logic circuit in which the output changes from one stable state to another when a pulse is applied to its input

fluctuation /ˌflʌktʃʊ'eɪʃn/ [5] small change above or below a fixed level

fluorescent lamp /flʊəˌresənt 'læmp/ [28] lighting device which uses a glass tube filled with a gas which emits light when struck by electrons

fluorescent tube /flʊəˌresənt 'tjuːb/ [28] gas filled glass tube used in a fluorescent lamp

flyback /'flaɪbæk/ [20] rapid movement of the spot on a CRT screen back to its starting position

FM /ˌef 'em/ [10] frequency-modulated

focus /'fəʊkəs/ [19] concentrate to give a clearer image

focus control /'fəʊkəs kənˌtrəʊl/ [19] control for making an image clearer

foil /fɔɪl/ [9] thin metal sheet

forward bias /ˌfɔːwəd 'baɪəs/ [9] DC control voltage which causes a component to pass more current

frame /freɪm/ [20] complete picture in a video display consisting of two fields

frame scan rate /'freɪm skæn reɪt/ [20] number of times per second that a video frame is displayed on a screen

frequency /'friːkwənsɪ/ [1] how often a pattern is repeated every second (measured in hertz, Hz)

frequency band /'friːkwənsɪ bænd/ [10] group of frequencies

frequency distribution /'friːkwənsɪ dɪstrɪˌbjuːʃn/ [27] spread of frequencies

frequency-modulated /ˌfriːkwənsɪ 'mɒdjʊleɪtɪd/ [10] with the frequency of the carrier wave varied according to the changing size of the signal being carried

frequency response /'friːkwənsɪ rɪˌspɒns/ [13] range of frequencies for which the audio signal level of an amplifier does not drop by more than 3dB

function generator /'fʌŋkʃn ˌdʒenəreɪtə(r)/ [3, 19] electronic device for producing various types of output signals (e.g. triangular, square, and sine waves) which can be used for the test and measurement of amplifiers

fuse /fjuːz/ [5] electrical component used as a safety device which heats up and melts, breaking the circuit when the current becomes too large

fuseholder /'fjuːzˌhəʊldə(r)/ [15] device for holding an electrical fuse

gain /geɪn/ n [11] amplification, measured by comparing the magnitude of the output of an amplifier with the magnitude of its input

generator /'dʒenəˌreɪtə(r)/ [12] device which produces electrical energy

germanium /dʒɜː'meɪnɪəm/ [16] chemical element (Ge) used to make semiconductor components

germanium diode /dʒɜː'meɪnɪəm ˌdaɪəʊd/ [15] electronic component made from germanium (Ge) which only allows current to flow in one direction

GHz /'dʒɪgəhɜːts/ [10] gigahertz (10^9 cycles per second)

glow /gləʊ/ [19] light given off by an object

gramophone /'græməfəʊn/ [16] *see* record player

gramophone record /'græməfəʊn ˌrekɔːd/ [16] vinyl disc used for storing audio recordings

graphic equalizer /ˌgræfɪk 'iːkwəlaɪzə(r)/ [13] electronic device which has slider controls for controlling the level of amplification of different frequencies

graphite /'græfaɪt/ [4] carbon material used in some resistors

graticule /ˈgræ kjʊəl/ [19] plastic grid placed over the display screen of an oscilloscope to allow measurements of the waveform to be made

ground /graʊnd/ [1] *see* earth

ground wave /ˈgraʊnd weɪv/ [10] radio wave which travels along the surface of the earth

handset /ˈhændset/ [8, 15] electronic device which can be held in one hand

harmonic wave /hɑːˌmɒnɪk ˈweɪv/ [13] part of a signal with a frequency which is a multiple of the basic fundamental frequency of the signal

HDTV /ˌeɪtʃ diː tiː ˈviː/ [20] High Definition Television

head /hed/ [12, 16] component where a magnetic or electric field is concentrated (usually for reading or writing to a magnetic tape or disc)

head drum /ˈhed drʌm/ [21] metal cylinder which holds the magnetic tape as it passes the record/playback head in a video recorder

headphones /ˈhedfəʊnz/ [15] device worn on the head which covers each ear with a small loudspeaker

headset /ˈhedset/ [12] attachment for holding headphones (and sometimes a microphone) on the user's head

hearing aid /ˈhɪərɪŋ eɪd/ [5] amplifying device which makes it easier for people with hearing difficulties to hear

heatsink /ˈhiːtsɪŋk/ [5] piece of metal used to allow the heat to escape from a component such as a transistor

Heaviside Layer, the /ðə ˈhevɪsaɪd ˌleɪə(r)/ *see* ionosphere

helical scanning /ˌhelɪkl ˈskænɪŋ/ [21] movement of a recorder head across the magnetic tape in a helix or corkscrew shaped path

hexagonal /hekˈsægənəl/ [27] six-sided

HF /ˌeɪtʃ ˈef/ [10] high frequency: frequency between 3MHz and 30MHz

hi-fi /ˈhaɪ faɪ/ [1, 13] high-fidelity: high quality sound reproduction which is true to the original sound

hi-tech /ˌhaɪ ˈtek/ [21] highly technical

Hi-Vision /ˌhaɪ ˈvɪʒn/ [20] name for new Japanese television system which provides clearer, more detailed, high quality images and very high quality sound

high logic level /ˌhaɪ ˈlɒdʒɪk ˌlevl/ [19] highest operating voltage of a digital logic circuit

High Definition Television /ˈhaɪ defɪˌnɪʃn ˈtelɪvɪʒn/ [20] name for new European television system which provides clearer, more detailed, high quality images and very high quality sound

hiss /hɪs/ [6, 13] background noise produced by magnetic tape or randomly produced inside electronic components

hopper /ˈhɒpə(r)/ [23] container used to hold materials and gradually feed them into a processing machine

hum /hʌm/ [12, 13] unwanted signals caused by induction from the power supply

hydraulic press /haɪˌdrɒlɪk ˈpres/ [23] machine operated using fluid pressure for cutting and shaping metal

Hz /hɜːts/ [12] hertz (cycles per second): basic unit of frequency

IC /ˌaɪ ˈsiː/ [1, 8] integrated circuit

impedance /ɪmˈpiːdəns/ [10] combined resistance to AC and DC

impulse /ˈɪmpʌls/ [15] a sudden rise or fall of voltage or current

in cascade /ɪŋ kæsˈkeɪd/ [24] connected so that the output of one circuit acts as the input to the next circuit

in parallel /ɪn ˈpærəlel/ [1] connected across each other

in series /ɪn ˈsɪərɪz/ [1] connected end to end

inch /ɪntʃ/ [21] British measurement equal to 2.54 centimetres

induce /ɪnˈdjuːs/ [10, 12] produce an electric or magnetic effect at a distance

inductance /ɪnˈdʌktəns/ [10] resistance to AC

induction /ɪnˈdʌkʃn/ [10, 12] production of an electric or magnetic effect at a distance

inductor /ɪnˈdʌktə(r)/ [1] coil which resists changes in voltage and current

information technology /ˌɪnfəmeɪʃn tekˈnɒlədʒɪ/ [2] the science of information, usually with regard to electronic systems and computers

infra-red /ˌɪnfrəˈred/ [8, 9] range of electromagnetic waves with wavelengths a little longer than that of red light (i.e. between 700nm and 1mm)

input /ˈɪnpʊt/ *n* [5] signal going into a circuit

insulated /ˈɪnsjʊˌleɪtɪd/ [26] covered by a material which does not conduct electricity

insulator /ˈɪnsjʊˌleɪtə(r)/ [26] material which does not allow current to flow

integrated circuit /ˌɪntɪgreɪtɪd ˈsɜːkɪt/ [1, 8] electronic circuit containing many components on a single silicon chip

Integrated Services Digital Network /ˌɪntɪgreɪtɪd ˌsɜːvɪsɪz ˌdɪdʒɪtl ˈnetwɜːk/ [28] system which interconnects all types of data communications networks throughout the world

intelligent terminal /ɪn'telɪdʒənt 'tɜːmɪnl/ [26] computer terminal which is capable of carrying out some processing on the data

intensity /ɪn'tensəti/ [19, 20] *see* brightness

interference /ɪntə'fɪərəns/ [8] unwanted signals

interlacing /'ɪntə,leɪsɪŋ/ [20] combining of video fields to make a frame by displaying the odd numbered lines of the frame followed by the even numbered lines

internal resistance /ɪn,tɜːnl rɪ'zɪstəns/ [5] the resistance inside a cell

international exchange /,ɪntənæʃnl ɪks'tʃeɪndʒ/ [28] telephone switching centre for connecting telephone lines between different countries

inverter /ɪn'vɜːtə(r)/ [23] *see* NOT gate

I/O /'aɪ 'əʊ/ [23] Input /Output in computer and data communications systems

ionized /'aɪənaɪzd/ [26] divided into charged particles

ionosphere, the /ðɪ aɪ'ɒnəs,fɪə(r)/ [10] layers of ionized gases and electrons in the earth's upper atmosphere which reflects radio waves

ISDN /,aɪ es diː 'en/ [28] Integrated Services Digital Network

IT /,aɪ 'tiː/ information technology

jack (plug) /dʒæk (plʌg)/ [26] type of plug used for making connections to telephone networks and audio circuits

jacket /'dʒækɪt/ [26] protective outer covering

jumping /'dʒʌmpɪŋ/ [16] sudden lifting of gramophone needle from one record track to another

key /kiː/ *n* [27] push switch

key in /kiː 'ɪn/ *v* [27, 28] press keys in the correct sequence

kHz /'kɪləhɜːts/ [10] kilohertz (thousands of cycles per second)

LAN /læn/ [29] local area network

LCD /,el siː 'diː/ [24] liquid crystal display

LDR /,el diː 'ɑː(r)/ [9] light dependent resistor

lead /liːd/ *n* [22] insulated wire for making a connection to an electrical device

leakage current /'liːkɪdʒ ,kʌrənt/ [18] unwanted current in a transistor

LED /,el iː 'diː/ [19] light-emitting diode

LF /,el 'ef/ [10] low frequency: frequency between 30kHz and 300kHz

light-dependent resistor /,laɪt dɪ,pendənt rɪ'zɪstə(r)/ [9] electronic component which varies its resistance depending on the amount of light falling on its surface

light-emitting diode /'laɪt ɪ,mɪtɪŋ 'daɪəʊd/ [8] semiconductor which converts electrical energy into light

line scan signal /'laɪn skæn ,sɪgnəl/ [20] part of a video signal which controls the movement of the spot across a television screen

line sync pulse /,laɪn sɪŋk pʌls/ [20] part of a video signal which adjusts the timing for the display of a line on a television screen

linear /'lɪnɪə(r)/ [21] varying in equal steps producing a straight line graph

liquid crystal display /,lɪkwɪd ,crɪstəl dɪs'pleɪ/ [24] thin film of liquid which displays different characters when a charge is applied to different parts of it

lithium /'lɪðɪəm/ [5] chemical element (Li) used in some batteries

live /laɪv/ *adj* [5] connected to the positive supply voltage

load /ləʊd/ *n* [5] component or device which is connected across the output of a circuit and dissipates power (e.g. loudspeaker, motor)

local area network /,ləʊkl ,eərɪə 'netwɜːk/ [29] interconnection of computers and terminals in a small area

local exchange /,ləʊkl ɪks'tʃeɪndʒ/ [28] telephone switching centre for connecting telephone lines in a small area

location engineer /ləʊ,keɪʃn endʒɪ'nɪə(r)/ [30] engineer who works on filming outside a studio

logarithmic scale /'lɒgərɪθmɪk skeɪl/ [13] scale of measurement which indicates the mathematical power to which a basic unit is raised

logic family /'lɒdʒɪk ,fæməlɪ/ [23] set of logic gates made from a particular type of semiconductor component

logic gate /'lɒdʒɪk geɪt/ [23] electronic switching circuit that operates according to mathematical rules of logic

logic level /'lɒdʒɪk ,levl/ [19, 23] *see* logic state

logic level 0 /,lɒdʒɪk ,levl 'zɪərəʊ/ [23] *see* low logic level

logic level 1 /,lɒdʒɪk ,levl 'wʌn/ [23] *see* high logic level

logic probe /'lɒdʒɪk prəʊb/ [19] electronic instrument used for detecting pulses and determining the logic level on the pins of logic chips

logic state /'lɒdʒɪk steɪt/ [24] one of two stable voltage levels of a digital circuit (i.e. 1 or 0, high or low)

long wave /'lɒŋ weɪv/ [10] range of radio signal wavelengths of more than one kilometre

long-play album /ˌlɒŋ pleɪ ˈælbəm/ [18] collection of recordings on a vinyl disc which plays for up to 45 minutes on each side

long-playing record /ˌlɒŋ pleɪɪŋ ˈrekɔːd/ [16] vinyl record which stores up to 45 minutes of audio recording on each side

loudness /ˈlaʊdnəs/ [15] *see* volume

loudspeaker /ˌlaʊdˈspiːkə(r)/ [1] device for converting electrical signals into sound

low logic level /ˌləʊ ˈlɒdʒɪk ˌlevl/ [19] lowest operating voltage of a digital logic circuit

LP /ˌel ˈpiː/ [16, 17] long-playing record

LSI /ˌel es ˈaɪ/ [23] large scale integration: between 100 and 1000 active components contained on one IC chip

M

mA /ˈmɪliæmps/ [11] milliamps

magnetic field /mæɡˌnetɪk ˈfiːld/ [12] area around a magnet in which the magnetic force has an effect

magnetic pick-up (head) /mæɡˌnetɪk ˈpɪk ʌp (hed)/ [13] part of a record player which uses electromagnetic induction to convert the movement of the gramophone needle into an electrical signal

magnetic tape /mæɡˌnetɪk ˈteɪp/ [21] plastic material coated in magnetic oxide used in thin strips for the magnetic storage of sound recordings

magnetism /ˈmæɡnəˌtɪzm/ [12] magnetic effects

magnetize /ˈmæɡnətaɪz/ [9] make a material magnetic

magneto-optical system /mæɡˌnetəʊ ˈɒptɪkl ˌsɪstəm/ [16] recording system which uses magnetism to store the data and laser light to guide the read/write head

magnitude /ˈmæɡnɪtjuːd/ [15] size given as a positive value

main switching centre /ˈmeɪn swɪtʃɪŋ ˌsentə(r)/ [27] cellular phone control station which uses a computer to control clusters and to connect them to the public telephone network

mains (supply), the /ðə ˈmeɪnz (səˌplaɪ)/ [5] common source of high voltage AC electricity provided throughout most buildings

mains cable /ˈmeɪnz ˌkeɪbl/ *see* mains lead

mains cord /ˈmeɪnz kɔːd/ [21] *see* mains lead

mains lead /ˈmeɪnz liːd/ [21] cable which connects an electrical device to the high voltage AC supply

mains outlet /ˈmeɪnz ˌaʊtlət/ [21] wall socket for connection to the main high voltage AC electricity supply

maintain /meɪnˈteɪn/ [22, 29] keep in good working order

maintenance /ˈmeɪntənəns/ [29] cleaning and adjusting of equipment to keep it in good working order

master /ˈmɑːstə(r)/ *n* [6] main recording which is used to produce many other copies

master /ˈmɑːstə(r)/ *v* [6] adjust the relative levels of each track when making an audio recording

master down /ˌmɑːstə ˈdaʊn/ [6] feed a multitrack recording back through a mixer to adjust the relative levels of each track

mastering machine /ˈmɑːstərɪŋ məˌʃiːn/ [6] machine used for producing master recordings

matrix (pl = matrices) /ˈmeɪtrɪks (ˈmeɪtrəsiːz)/ [8] complex arrangement of wires which cross over each other at 90°

MD /ˌem ˈdiː/ [6, 16] MiniDisc

medium wave /ˈmiːdiəm weɪv/ [10] range of radio signal wavelengths between approximately 100m and 1000m

memory /ˈmeməri/ [15] electronic circuit for storing information

mercury switch /ˈmɜːkjʊri swɪtʃ/ [9] electrical switch which uses the movement of mercury to make or break the contacts

metal detector /ˈmetl dɪˌtektə(r)/ [12] electronic device for indicating the presence of metal objects under the ground

MF /ˌem ˈef/ [10] medium frequency: frequency between 300kHz and 3MHz

MHz /ˈmegəhɜːts/ [10, 11] megahertz (millions of cycles per second)

microchip /ˈmaɪkrəʊtʃɪp/ [8] small electronic component which contains an integrated circuit on one piece of silicon

microcomputer /ˌmaɪkrəʊkəmˈpjuːtə(r)/ [23] small personal computer

microelectronics /ˌmaɪkrəʊelekˈtrɒnɪks/ [1] electronics using integrated circuits

millihenry /ˈmɪlihenri/ [1] one thousandth of a henry (mH): measure of inductance

microphone /ˈmaɪkrəfəʊn/ [1, 6] device for converting sound waves into electrical signals

microprocessor /maɪkrəʊˈprəʊsesə(r)/ [1, 23] IC chip at the centre of a computer for controlling the system and processing the data

micro system /ˈmaɪkrəʊ ˌsɪstəm/ [30] microprocessor system: system which uses a microprocessor

microwave /ˈmaɪkrəʊweɪv/ [9] electromagnetic wave with very short wavelength (i.e. between 135cm and a fraction of a millimetre)

mid-fi system /ˈmɪd faɪ ˌsɪstəm/ [13] medium quality sound reproduction

mike /maɪk/ [7, 28] *see* microphone

milliammeter /ˈmɪlɪˈæmɪtə(r)/ [5] electronic instrument for measuring small currents (i.e. thousandths of an amp)

MiniDisc /ˈmɪnɪ dɪsk/ [16] small magneto-optical disk used to digitally store high quality sound recordings

mix /mɪks/ [6] combine input signals from different sources

mix down /mɪks ˈdaʊn/ [7] *see* master down

mixer /ˈmɪksə(r)/ [6] electronic circuit for combining input signals from different sources

mixing desk /ˈmɪksɪŋ desk/ [6] desk containing electronic circuits for combining signals from different sources

mobile phone /ˌməʊbaɪl ˈfəʊn/ [27] portable radio telephone that can be used while the user is moving

modem /ˈməʊdem/ [26, 28] modulator demodulator: electronic device used by computers for converting outgoing signals from digital to analogue form and incoming signals from analogue to digital form

modulate /ˈmɒdjʊleɪt/ [1] combine a signal with a carrier wave

modulation /ˌmɒdjʊˌleɪʃn/ [10] shaping of a carrier wave by combining it with a signal to be carried

modulator /ˈmɒdjʊˌleɪtə(r)/ [1] electronic circuit for combining a signal with a carrier wave

Morse code, the /ðə ˌmɔːs ˈkəʊd/ [26] early system of coded signals consisting of short and long pulses (dots and dashes) for transmitting messages by telegraph

mouthpiece /ˈmaʊθpiːs/ [26] part of a telephone which contains a small microphone and is held near the user's mouth

MSC /ˌem es ˈsiː/ [27] main switching centre

MSC register /ˌem es ˈsiː ˈredʒɪstə(r)/ [27] stored information indicating the position of each cellphone

MSI /ˌem es ˈaɪ/ [23] medium scale integration: between 10 and 100 active components on one IC chip

mu-metal /ˈmjuː metl/ [19] alloy of nickel (Ni) with a high magnetic permeability. Used as a casing for cathode ray tubes to prevent interference from external magnetic fields.

multi-frequency dialling /ˈmʌltɪ ˌfriːkwənsɪ ˈdaɪəlɪŋ/ [26] system used on modern digital telephones for dialling a number in which each telephone push-button generates an audio signal of a different frequency

multimedia /ˌmʌltɪˈmiːdɪə/ [1] system which uses a combination of different media (e.g. sound, graphics, video)

multimeter /ˈmʌltɪˌmiːtə(r)/ [19] electronic instrument for measuring various electrical quantities including voltage, current and resistance

multitrack /ˈmʌltɪˌtræk/ [6] sound recording in which the different sounds which make up the recording are recorded on separate tracks

music centre /ˈmjuːzɪk ˌsentə(r)/ [13] unit containing a combination of sound reproduction devices such as a tape deck, a radio tuner, a CD player, an amplifier, loudspeakers etc.

mW /ˈmɪlɪwɒts/ [11] milliwatt (thousandths of a watt): measure of power

NAND gate /ˈnænd geɪt/ [23] digital logic gate which has a high output unless all its inputs are high

natural frequency /ˌnætʃərəl ˈfriːkwənsɪ/ *see* resonant frequency

neon lamp /ˌniːɒn ˈlæmp/ [5] electrical component which gives off light when a voltage ionizes the neon gas inside

network /ˈnetwɜːk/ [26] system of interconnected devices

network manager /ˌnetwɜːk ˈmænɪdʒə(r)/ [29] person in charge of the operation of a computer network

NiCad /ˈnɪkæd/ [5] nickel cadmium (NiCd): chemical used is some batteries

noise /nɔɪz/ [8, 13] *see* interference

noisy /ˈnɔɪzɪ/ [28] affected by unwanted signals

NOT gate /ˈnɒt geɪt/ [23] digital logic gate which has a high output when its input is low and vice versa

NPN transistor /ˌen piː ˈen trænˌzɪstə(r)/ [1, 11] type of transistor made from a thin layer of P-type semiconductor material between two thicker layers of N-type semiconductor material

ohm /ˈəʊm/ [1] unit of resistance (Ω)

ohmmeter /ˈəʊmmiːtə(r)/ [19] electronic instrument for measuring resistance

op amp /ˈɒp æmp/ [1] *see* operational amplifier

open /ˈəʊpn/ [11] unconnected

operational amplifier /ˌɒpəreɪʃənl ˈæmplɪfaɪə(r)/ [1] an extremely high gain analogue IC amplifier

optical fibre /ˌɒptɪkl ˈfaɪbə(r)/ [26, 28] strand of silica for guiding light waves

optical flatness /ˌɒptɪkl ˈflætnəs/ [6] flat enough to give accurate deflection of light

optoelectronics /ˌɒptəʊelekˈtrɒnɪks/ [2] the study and use of optical components in electronics

OR gate /ˈɔː(r) geɪt/ [23] digital logic gate which has a high output when any of its inputs are high

oscillate /ˈɒsɪleɪt/ [10] move backwards and forwards between two different states

oscillator /ˈɒsɪleɪtə(r)/ [1] electronic circuit which produces a repeating signal

oscilloscope /ɒˈsɪləskəʊp/ [19] *see* cathode ray oscilloscope

outer space /ˌaʊtə ˈspeɪs/ [10] region beyond the earth's atmosphere

output /ˈaʊtpʊt/ *n* [1] signal coming out of a circuit

P

page /peɪdʒ/ *v* [27] send a signal to indicate that a message is waiting to be communicated

pager /ˈpeɪdʒə(r)/ [28, 30] *see* radiopager

paging system /ˈpeɪdʒɪŋ ˌsɪstəm/ [30] mobile communications system which uses pager devices to contact people

panning /ˈpænɪŋ/ [15] steady movement of the apparent source of sound across an area

parallel wire cable /ˌpærəlel ˈwaɪə ˌkeɪbl/ [26] transmission line consisting of two wires running side-by-side and covered by an insulating material

passive infra-red detector /ˌpæsɪv ɪnfrəˈred dɪˌtektə(r)/ [9] device which detects the presence of heat given off by a body

PCB /ˌpiː siː ˈbiː/ printed circuit board

PCM /ˌpiː siː ˈem/ [26] pulse code modulation: modulation system which sends a differently coded train of pulses to represent each size of sampled signal

PD /ˌpiː ˈdiː/ potential difference: *see* voltage drop

peak point /ˈpiːk pɔɪnt/ [18] highest turning value on a curved graph

permeability /ˌpɜːmɪəˈbɪləti/ [19] property of a material which measures the ratio of flux density to magnetic field strength

personal stereo /ˌpɜːsənl ˈsteriəʊ/ [18] small portable cassette tape player with stereo sound designed for use by one person

perspex /ˈpɜːspeks/ [6, 16] tough transparent plastic material used to make compact discs

phone /fəʊn/ [26, 28] *see* telephone

phones /fəʊnz/ [28] *see* headphones

phono socket /ˈfəʊnəʊ ˌsɒkɪt/ [22] common type of connector used on audio devices

phosphor /ˈfɒsfə(r)/ [19] metal compound which gives off light when hit by a stream of electrons

photodiode /ˌfəʊtəʊ ˈdaɪəʊd/ [4, 8] semiconductor which is sensitive to light causing a reverse current to flow when light shines on it

photoresist /ˌfəʊtəʊrɪˈzɪst/ [6, 17] chemical lacquer which is sensitive to light and is used in making compact discs and printed circuit boards

picofarad /ˈpɪkəʊˈfæræd/ [1] 10^{-12} of a farad (pF): measure of capacitance

piezoelectric crystal /ˌpiːzəʊɪlektrɪk ˈkrɪstəl/ *see* quartz crystal

pin /pɪn/ [19] input or output connector of an IC chip

pin-out diagram /ˌpɪnaʊt ˈdaɪəɡræm/ [23] diagram showing the function and signal level of each pin of an IC chip

pit /pɪt/ [6, 16] hollow area produced on the surface of a compact disc by a laser beam

pitch /pɪtʃ/ [28] frequency level

plate /pleɪt/ American term for anode

playback /ˈpleɪbæk/ [7] playing of a recording

PN junction /ˌpiː en ˈdʒʌŋkʃən/ [18] surface where a layer of N-type and a layer of P-type semiconductor meet

PNP transistor /ˌpiː en ˈpiː trænˈzɪstə(r)/ [1, 11] type of transistors made from a thin layer of N-type semiconductor material between two thicker layers of P-type semiconductor material

pole /pəʊl/ [5] positive or negative terminal

polyethylene /ˌpɒlɪˈeθəliːn/ [26] translucent plastic insulating material used as a dielectric in coaxial cable

polythene /ˈpɒləθiːn/ *see* polyethylene

Portastudio /ˈpɔːtəˌstjuːdɪəʊ/ [7] portable recording studio

pot /pɒt/ [1] *see* potentiometer

potential difference /pəˌtenʃl ˈdɪfrəns/ *see* voltage drop

potential divider /pəˌtenʃl dɪˈvaɪdə(r)/ [9] part of an electronic circuit which divides a voltage into two or more smaller parts

potentiometer /pəˌtensɪˈɒmɪtə(r)/ [1] variable electronic component for dividing a voltage into two smaller parts

power amp /ˈpaʊər æmp/ [1, 13] *see* power amplifier

power amplifier /ˈpaʊər ˌæmplɪfaɪə(r)/ [13] electronic circuit used to increase the power of audio signals to enable them to drive loudspeaker systems

power cut /ˈpaʊə kʌt/ [9] sudden failure of the main power supply

power dissipation /ˈpaʊə ˌdɪsɪˌpeɪʃn/ [23] gradual release of energy over a period of time

power rating /ˈpaʊə ˌreɪtɪŋ/ [18] manufacturer's recommended maximum operating power for a component

power transistor /ˈpaʊə trænˌzɪstə(r)/ [13] large transistor used in a power amplifier for increasing the power of a signal

pre-amp /ˈpriːæmp/ [11] *see* preamplifier

preamplifier /priːˈæmplɪˌfaɪə(r)/ [13] electronic circuit used to increase audio signal voltage

preferred values /prɪˈfɜːd ˌvæljuːz/ [4] set of standard values from which all other values can be produced

pressure mat /ˈpreʃə mæt/ [9] rubber mat switch used in alarm systems to detect a change of pressure caused by someone stepping on the mat

primary /ˈpraɪmərɪ/ n [5] transformer input coil

primary cell /ˌpraɪmərɪ ˈsel/ [5] energy source which cannot be recharged

printed circuit /ˌprɪntɪd ˈsɜːkɪt/ [14] circuit with conductors printed and etched on a copper board

program /ˈprəʊɡræm/ n [23] set of instructions for controlling a computer

programme /ˈprəʊɡræm/ n [20] television/radio show

programmer /ˈprəʊɡræmə(r)/ [29] person who writes computer programs

propagation /ˌprɒpəˌɡeɪʃn/ [10] movement of a signal through a medium such as air or water

PSTN /ˌpiː es tiː ˈen/ [28] Public Switching Telephone Network

Public Switching Telephone Network /ˌpʌblɪk ˌswɪtʃɪŋ ˈteləfəʊn ˌnetwɜːk/ [28] national system of interconnected telephone lines for use by the general public

public telephone exchange /ˌpʌblɪk ˈteləfəʊn ɪksˌtʃeɪndʒ/ [27] switching centre in a public telephone network which switches the signals from one line to another

puff /pʌf/ [1, 28] see picofarad (pF)

pulse /pʌls/ [12] a sudden increase then decrease in voltage or current

pulsed /pʌlst/ [8] in the form of a rectangular wave with short duration

push-pull configuration /pʊʃ ˈpʊl kənfɪɡəˌreɪʃn/ [13] circuit arrangement in which each half of the circuit is 180° out of phase with the other half. It allows the complete cycle of a signal to be used for driving loudspeakers.

PVC /ˌpiː viː ˈsiː/ [26] polyvinyl chloride: plastic insulating material used to protect some cables

quartz crystal /ˈkwɔːts ˌkrɪstəl/ [19] naturally occurring silicon oxide crystal which vibrates at a fixed frequency when an AC voltage is applied to it. It is used in oscillators to produce a very stable resonant frequency.

R and D /ˌɑːr ən ˈdiː/ [29] research and development

radar /ˈreɪdɑː(r)/ [8, 26] radio detection and ranging: electronic system which uses the reflection of microwaves to detect the presence of an object and measure its distance and position relative to the transmitter

radiate /ˈreɪdɪeɪt/ [26] give out rays in all directions

radiation /ˌreɪdɪˈeɪʃn/ [8] electromagnetic wave sent out in all directions

radio (set) /ˈreɪdɪəʊ (ˌset)/ [1] device for receiving radio frequency signals

radio frequency /ˈreɪdɪəʊ ˌfriːkwənsɪ/ [10] frequency between 100kHz and 300GHz

radio phone /ˈreɪdɪəʊ ˌfəʊn/ [27] telephone which transmits and receives radio frequency signals

radio receiver /ˈreɪdɪəʊ rɪˌsiːvə(r)/ see radio (set)

radio tuner /ˈreɪdɪəʊ ˌtjuːnə(r)/ [13] part of a radio receiver for selecting the desired radio programme

radiopager /ˈreɪdɪəʊ ˌpeɪdʒə(r)/ [28] mobile radio communications device which beeps to let the user know that someone is trying to contact them

radiopaging /ˈreɪdɪəʊˌpeɪdʒɪŋ/ [28] communications service using radio pager devices which beep to let the user know that someone is trying to get in contact with them

radiopaging system /ˌreɪdɪəʊ ˈpeɪdʒɪŋ ˌsɪstəm/ see paging system

RAM /ræm/ [23] random-access memory

random access /ˌrændəm ˈækses/ [16, 23] access to any area of a recording without having to go through other recorded areas

random-access memory /ˈrændəm ˈækses ˌmemərɪ/ [23] IC chips used in computers for the temporary storage of programs and data. Data can be both written to and read from them.

range /reɪndʒ/ n **1** [6] selection between an upper and lower limit **2** [10] the maximum distance a wave can travel

ranging /ˈreɪndʒɪŋ/ n [29] process of calculating how far away an object is

raster pattern /ˈræstəˌpætən/ [20] scan path of an electron beam going across and down the screen of a television receiver

ray /reɪ/ [19] narrow beam of light

read-only memory /riːd ˈəʊnlɪ ˌmemərɪ/ [15, 23] IC chips used in computers for storing fixed programs and data. The user's data can be read from them but not written to them.

realign /ˌriːəˈlaɪn/ [24] go back into line with

receiver /rɪˈsiːvə(r)/ [8] electronic circuit for receiving signals

reception /rɪˈsepʃn/ [21] receiving of transmitted signals

recharge /ˌriːˈtʃɑːdʒ/ [5] restore the charge or energy to a battery

record /ˈrekɔːd/ n [6, 16] see gramophone record

record /rɪ'kɔːd/ v [6] make a recording

record player /'rekɔːd ˌpleɪə(r)/ [1] device for playing vinyl record recordings

recorder /rɪ'kɔːdə(r)/ [6] machine use to record sound or video signals on magnetic tape

recording /rɪ'kɔːdɪŋ/ [6] sound or video signals stored on a disc or tape

recording studio /rɪ'kɔːdɪŋ ˌstjuːdɪəʊ/ [14] place where recordings are made

rectifier /'rektɪfaɪə(r)/ [5] electronic circuit for changing AC into DC

rectify /'rektɪfaɪ/ [5] change AC into DC

redial /ˌriː'daɪəl/ [26] memory function on modern telephones which can be used to automatically dial a telephone number again

reed switch /'riːd swɪtʃ/ [9] small electrical switch enclosed in a glass tube which operates when a magnet is brought close to it

reel /riːl/ [21] circular holder for magnetic tape

reel-to-reel machine /riːl tə 'riːl məˈʃiːn/ [21] tape recorder which moves the magnetic tape off one reel on to another reel as it passes the heads

reflected wave /rɪ'flektɪd weɪv/ see sky wave

reflection /rɪ'flekʃn/ [10] change of direction of a wave after hitting a surface

reflective /rɪ'flektɪv/ [24] causing reflection

reflector /rɪ'flektə(r)/ [10] device that reflects energy

relay /'riːleɪ/ n [9] electromechanical switch operated by an electromagnet

relay /rɪ'leɪ/ v [27] pass on a signal

remote control (unit) /rɪˌməʊt kən'trəʊl (ˌjuːnɪt)/ [8] device for controlling equipment from a distance

reset /ˌriː'set/ v [9] restore to starting condition

resistance /rɪ'zɪstəns/ [5] opposition to the flow of charge

resistivity /ˌriːzɪs'tɪvɪti/ [24] resistance property of a material which depends only on the type of material and not on its size

resistor /rɪ'zɪstə(r)/ [1, 4] electronic component for opposing the flow of charge

resonant circuit /'rezənənt ˌsɜːkɪt/ see tuned circuit

resonant frequency /'rezənənt ˌfriːkwənsi/ [10] frequency at which a tuned circuit will naturally oscillate

reverb /'riːvɜːb/ n [6, 7] see reverberation

reverberation /rɪˌvɜːbəˌreɪʃn/ [6, 7] artificial echo effect produced by electronically delaying the sound signal

reverse bias /rɪˌvɜːs 'baɪəs/ [9] DC control voltage which causes a component to pass less current

(reverse) breakdown voltage /(rɪˌvɜːs) 'breɪkdaʊn ˌvɒltɪdʒ/ [18] see zener voltage

rewind motor /rɪ'waɪnd ˌməʊtə(r)/ [22] electric motor for winding back the magnetic tape in a recorder

RF /ˌɑːr 'ef/ [1] radio frequency

ringing tone /'rɪŋɪŋ təʊn/ [27] telephone sound which indicates that a line has been connected and the system is waiting for the person receiving the call to lift up the phone

robot /'rəʊbɒt/ [1] machine controlled by a computer

robotics /rəʊ'bɒtɪks/ [29] study and application of computer-controlled machines

ROM /rɒm/ [15, 23] read-only memory

S/N ratio /es 'en ˌreɪʃɪəʊ/ [13] signal-to-noise ratio

sample /'sɑːmpl/ n [15] the part of a signal which is measured at a particular instant of time and used to convert analogue sound signals into their digital equivalent

sample /'sɑːmpl/ v [15] measure a signal at particular moments of time

sampling /'sɑːmplɪŋ/ [15] method of measuring the magnitude of an analogue signal at different points of time to enable it to be converted to an equivalent digital signal

satellite /'sætəlaɪt/ [10, 26] telecommunications device which circles the earth to receive, amplify, and retransmit signals around the world

satellite receiver /'sætəlaɪt rɪˌsiːvə(r)/ [29] electronic device for receiving microwave signals transmitted from a satellite

saturation /'sætjʊˌreɪʃn/ [9] state of a component in which it can produce no further change in response when the controlling signal continues to change

sawtooth waveform /ˌsɔːtuːθ 'weɪvfɔːm/ [19] waveform with each cycle having the shape of a triangle

scale of integration /ˌskeɪl əv ˌɪntɪ'greɪʃn/ [23] measurement of the number of active components contained on one IC chip

scan /skæn/ v [19, 20] move a signal steadily across an area

schematic /skɪ'mætɪk/ American term for circuit diagram

scope /skəʊp/ see cathode ray oscilloscope

screen /skriːn/ n [12, 19] surface on which an image is displayed (e.g. display area of a cathode ray tube)

screen /skriːn/ v [26] shield from electrical interference

search coil /'sɜːtʃ kɔɪl/ [12] coil of wire for detecting a change in an electromagnetic field due to the presence of a metal object

secondary cell /ˌsekəndri 'sel/ [5] energy source which can be recharged

self-contained /ˌself kənˈteɪnd/ [25] complete in itself without the need for outside help

semiconductor /ˌsemɪkənˈdʌktə(r)/ [23] component made from a material which changes from being an insulator to being a conductor when certain impurities are added to it

sensor /ˈsensə(r)/ [9, 16] device which produces an electrical signal when it detects a particular form of energy

serial access /ˌsɪərɪəl ˈækses/ [16] access to one recorded area after another in order starting with the first recorded area

service /ˈsɜːvɪs/ [29] carry out routine maintenance

sheath /ʃiːθ/ [26] close-fitting protective covering

SHF /ˌes eɪtʃ ˈef/ [10] super high frequency: frequency above 3GHz

short wave /ˈʃɔːt weɪv/ [10] range of radio signal wavelengths between approximately 10m and 100m

signal /ˈsɪgnəl/ [1] pattern of electricity used to send information

signal generator /ˈsɪgnəl ˌdʒenəreɪtə(r)/ [19] electronic device which produces various signals used in the test and measurement of amplifiers

signal-to-noise ratio /ˌsɪgnəl tə ˈnɔɪz ˌreɪʃɪəʊ/ [13] comparison of the level of the wanted part of a signal with the unwanted part

silica /ˈsɪlɪkə/ [26] silicon dioxide (SiO_2): used to make optical fibre cables

silicon /ˈsɪlɪkən/ [1] chemical element (Si) used to make semiconductor components

silicon diode /ˌsɪlɪkən ˈdaɪəʊd/ [15] electronic component made from silicon (Si) which only allows current to flow in one direction

sine wave /ˈsaɪn weɪv/ [15] wave in the shape of a smooth curve which shows the relationship between an angle and its mathematical sine ratio

single (record) /ˈsɪŋgl (ˌrekɔːd)/ [18] vinyl record with only one piece of music recorded on each side

sky wave /ˈskaɪ weɪv/ [10] radio wave which travels upwards to the ionosphere where it is reflected back down towards Earth

slanted /ˈslɑːntɪd/ [21] at an angle to

slider /ˈslaɪdə(r)/ [13] see wiper

SLSI /ˌes el es ˈaɪ/ [23] super large scale integration: between 10^4 and 10^5 active components contained on one IC chip

smoke alarm /ˈsməʊk əˌlɑːm/ [15] device which gives a warning when it detects smoke

smoothing circuit /ˈsmuːðɪŋ ˌsɜːkɪt/ [5] electronic circuit for removing fluctuations in DC

snow /snəʊ/ [21] interference to a video signal which causes small marks to appear across the displayed image

software /ˈsɒftweə(r)/ [29] programs and data used in computing

sound baffle /ˈsaʊnd bæfl/ [13] wall within a loudspeaker unit for absorbing the sound coming from the back of the loudspeaker cone to prevent it cancelling out the sound coming from the front of the cone

sound track /ˈsaʊnd træk/ [20] magnetic area where the sound signals are stored on a recorded tape

space wave /ˈspeɪs weɪv/ [10] unguided wave which travels in a straight line through free space

speaker /ˈspiːkə(r)/ [13, 19] see loudspeaker

speaker system /ˈspiːkə ˌsɪstəm/ [13] set of loudspeakers and their associated electronic circuits

spec /spek/ see specification

specification /ˌspesɪfɪˈkeɪʃn/ [21] design detail

spot /spɒt/ [19, 20] small circle of light which is moved across a cathode ray tube screen to build up a video image

square wave /ˈskweə weɪv/ [19] waveform with each cycle having the shape of a square

squawker /ˈskwɔːkə(r)/ [13] medium-sized loudspeaker used for medium frequency audio signals

SSI /ˌes es ˈaɪ/ [23] small scale integration: up to 10 active components contained on one IC chip

stabilising circuit /ˈsteɪbəlaɪzɪŋ ˌsɜːkɪt/ [5] electronic circuit which prevents the voltage level from varying

stable /ˈsteɪbl/ [24] in a balanced state

stage /steɪdʒ/ [5] circuit block: section of an electronic circuit with a specific function

standby /ˈstændbaɪ/ [27] mode in which a device is waiting to receive a signal

static /ˈstætɪk/ n [16] electric charge produced by friction due to rubbing

static /ˈstætɪk/ adj [21] fixed, not moving

step down /step ˈdaʊn/ [5] reduce in magnitude

step up /step ˈʌp/ [5] increase in magnitude

stereo /ˈsterɪəʊ/ [6] having signals for the left- and right-hand speakers recorded as two separate channels

submarine cable /ˌsʌbməˈriːn ˈkeɪbl/ [26] transmission line laid under water on the ocean floor

supply rail /səˈplaɪ ˈreɪl/ [1] conductor for feeding the supply voltage to components in a circuit

suppress /səˈpres/ [18] prevent a signal getting through

surface wave /ˈsɜːfɪs weɪv/ [9, 10] see ground wave

surge /sɜːdʒ/ [23] sudden increase in amplitude of current or voltage

surge suppressor /'sɜːdʒ sə,presə(r)/ [13] electronic circuit for smoothing out sudden large changes in current or voltage

switch /swɪtʃ/ [5] electrical component for opening and closing a circuit

switchboard /'swɪtʃbɔːd/ [26] telephone switching centre where a person controls the switching of lines

sync /sɪŋk/ [20] synchronization: adjustment of the timing of signals so that they are in step with each other (i.e. they start at the same time)

systems approach /'sɪstəmz ə,prəʊtʃ/ [1] way of considering a circuit by focusing on the function of each stage

take-up reel /'teɪk ʌp ,riːl/ [21] tape recorder reel which gathers the magnetic tape after it has passed the heads

tamper sensor /'tæmpə(r) ,sensə(r)/ [9] device which detects when someone is interfering with a piece of equipment

tape-loading rollers /'teɪp ,ləʊdɪŋ ,rəʊləz/ [21] small metal or rubber cylinders in a recorder for pulling magnetic tape past the heads

tape recorder /'teɪp rɪ,kɔːdə(r)/ [1] machine for recording sound using magnetic tape

telecommunications /,telɪkəmjuːnɪ'keɪʃnz/ [26] transmission and reception of signals over long distances

telegraphy /tə'legrəfɪ/ [26] transmission of coded electrical signals over long distances

telemetry /tə'lemətrɪ/ [25] electronic measurement at a distance

telephone /'telɪfəʊn/ [1, 26] communications device which enables one person to speak to another over long distances

telephone exchange /'telɪfəʊn ɪks,tʃeɪndʒ/ [28] switching centre for switching signals from one telephone line to another

telephone line /'telɪfəʊn laɪn/ [26, 28] set of cables used to carry telephone signals

telephone network /'telɪfəʊn ,netwɜːk/ [15] system of interconnected telephones

telephone traffic /'telɪfəʊn ,træfɪk/ [26] signals travelling along telephone lines

telephony /tə'lefənɪ/ [26] transmission of speech over long distances

teleprinter /'telɪ,prɪntə(r)/ [28] device used for printing received telex messages

teletex /'telɪteks/ [28] modern telex communications service for transmitting text and graphics over long distances

teletext /'telɪtekst/ [8, 28] communications service which transmits text and graphics

over long distances as part of a television video signal

teletype terminal /'telɪtaɪp ,tɜːmɪnəl/ [28] device used for sending telex messages

television /'telɪvɪʒn/ [1, 14] communications system for the transmission and reception of video images over long distances

television (set) /'telɪvɪʒn (,set)/ [20] electronic device for receiving video images over long distances

television receiver /'telɪvɪʒn rɪ,siːvə(r)/ [20] see television (set)

television station /'telɪvɪʒn ,steɪʃn/ [20] television channel

telex /'teleks/ [26, 28] communications service for transmitting simple text over long distances

terminal /'tɜːmɪnəl/ **1** [1] part of an electronic component or circuit where leads can be attached **2** [26] input/output device connected to a computer network

THD /,tiː eɪtʃ 'diː/ [13] total harmonic distortion

thermal /'θɜːməl/ [28] to do with heat

thermionic valve /,θɜːmɪɒnɪk 'vælv/ [26] electronic component which was commonly used before the invention of semiconductor devices such as transistors. A small heater drives electrons from the surface of an electrode inside a vacuum glass tube.

thermistor /'θɜːmɪstə(r)/ [9] resistor made from a semiconductor material which is very sensitive to heat, decreasing its resistance as it gets warmer

tilt /tɪlt/ v [9] move to a sloping position by lifting one end

timebase generator /'taɪmbeɪs ,dʒənəreɪtə(r)/ [19] electronic circuit which produces a sawtooth wave to control the speed of the spot across the screen of a cathode ray tube

tolerance /'tɒlərens/ [4] amount of acceptable variation

tone /təʊn/ [26] audio signal of a particular frequency used in modern digital telephone systems for dialling a telephone number

tone control /'təʊn kən,trəʊl/ [13] control for adjusting the range of frequencies to be amplified

tone generator /'təʊn ,dʒenəreɪtə(r)/ [26] electronic circuit for generating coded audio signals which are used in modern digital telephone systems for dialling a number

torch /tɔːtʃ/ [5] portable electrical device for producing a beam of light

total harmonic distortion /,təʊtl hɑː'mɒnɪk dɪs'tɔːʃn/ [13] overall effect of the generation of unwanted harmonic waves in an amplifier by such effects as clipping

track /træk/ [6] narrow area on a disc or tape where recordings are stored

transceiver /træn'siːvə(r)/ [27] device which is a combined transmitter and receiver

transducer /trænz'djuːsə(r)/ [9] component which converts energy from one form to another

transformer /træns'fɔːmə(r)/ [5] component consisting of two or more coils of wire for increasing, decreasing or isolating an AC supply voltage

transistor /træn'zɪstə(r)/ [1] semiconductor component with three electrodes (emitter, base and collector) used for switching or amplifying an electronic signal

transistor-transistor logic /træn'zɪstə træn'zɪstə ˌlɒdʒɪk/ [23] family of integrated circuits containing various combinations of bipolar transistors

transmission /trænz'mɪʃn/ [15] signal sent from one point to another

transmission line /trænz'mɪʃn laɪn/ [26, 28] cable or duct for guiding signals between two points

transmit /trænz'mɪt/ [5] send a signal

transmitter /trænz'mɪtə(r)/ [1] electronic circuit for sending out signals

transparent /træns'pærənt/ [19] allowing light to pass through

transport mechanism /'trænspɔːt ˌmekənɪzm/ [21] mechanical device for moving the magnetic tape in a recorder

treble /'trebl/ [6] high frequency sounds

triangular wave /traɪ'æŋɡjʊlə weɪv/ [19] waveform with each cycle having the shape of an equilateral triangle

trigger /'trɪɡə(r)/ [9] short signal which causes a process to be started

trimmer /'trɪmə(r)/ [11] small, preset, variable capacitor or resistor for making fine adjustments in a circuit

trip (a switch) /trɪp (ə 'swɪtʃ)/ v [9] cause a switch to operate

troubleshooter /'trʌblˌʃuːtə(r)/ [27] person whose job it is to solve problems quickly

troubleshooting chart /'trʌblʃuːtɪŋ tʃɑːt/ [21] diagram to help find and solve the cause of a problem in a piece of equipment

trunk exchange /'trʌŋk ɪksˌtʃeɪndʒ/ [28] telephone switching centre for connecting local exchanges to each other and to international exchanges

trunk telephone line /ˌtrʌŋk 'telɪfəʊn laɪn/ [26] main telephone transmission line connecting one local exchange to another

truth table /'truːθ ˌteɪbl/ [23] table showing the output of a logic gate for all the possible combinations of its inputs

TTL /ˌtiː tiː 'el/ [23] transistor–transistor logic

tune /tjuːn/ [5, 15] adjust a circuit to oscillate at a particular frequency

tuned /tjuːnd/ [10] adjusted to oscillate at a particular frequency

tuned circuit /'tjuːnd ˌsɜːkɪt/ [1] electronic circuit which oscillates at a particular resonant frequency when fed by an AC signal

tuner /'tjuːnə(r)/ [1, 10] part of a receiver circuit consisting of an aerial and a tuned circuit (may also include a demodulator)

tunnel diode /ˌtʌnəl 'daɪəʊd/ [14] PN junction semiconductor which oscillates when suitably biased. Used as a low power microwave oscillator for radar.

turntable /'tɜːnˌteɪbl/ [13] circular revolving surface in a record player on which a vinyl record is played

TV /ˌtiː 'viː/ [20] television

tweeter /'twiːtə(r)/ [13] small loudspeaker used for high frequency audio signals

twisted pair /ˌtwɪstɪd 'peə(r)/ [26, 28] transmission line consisting of a set of two insulated copper wires twisted together to keep unwanted signal noise to a minimum

UHF /juː eɪtʃ 'ef/ [10] ultra-high frequency: frequency between 300MHz and 3GHz

ultrasonic /ˌʌltrə'sɒnɪk/ [9] having a frequency which is just above the audible range (i.e. between 20kHz and 5MHz)

unenergized /ˌʌn'enədʒaɪzd/ [13] with no energy having been provided

V /viː/ [4, 11] volt

vacuum tube /'vækjuːm tjuːb/ [1] American term for thermionic valve

valley point /'vælɪ pɔɪnt/ [18] lowest turning point on a curved graph

valve /vælv/ [1] see thermionic valve

variable capacitor /ˌveəriəbl kə'pæsɪtə(r)/ [1] capacitor with a capacitance that can be changed mechanically

variable resistor /ˌveəriəbl rɪ'zɪstə(r)/ [5] resistor with a resistance that can be changed mechanically

VCR /ˌviː siː 'ɑː(r)/ [21] video cassette recorder

VDU /ˌviː diː 'juː/ [28] visual (or video) display unit: computer terminal with a video screen

VDU terminal /ˌviː diː 'juː ˌtɜːmɪnəl/ [28] device with CRT screen and keyboard used for sending teletex messages

verify /'verɪfaɪ/ [8] test for accuracy

VHF /ˌviː eɪtʃ 'ef/ [10] very high frequency: frequency between 30MHz and 300MHz

VHS tape /ˌviː eɪtʃ 'es teɪp/ [21] most common type of video tape cassette used in video recorders

vibrate /vaɪˈbreɪt/ [13] move rapidly backwards and forwards

vibration sensor /vaɪˈbreɪʃn ˌsensə(r)/ [9] device for detecting small movements

video /ˈvɪdɪəʊ/ *adj* [1, 20] to do with the transmission and reception of images

video cassette recorder /ˌvɪdɪəʊ kəˈset rɪˌkɔːdə(r)/ [21] device for playing and recording video images using magnetic tape

Video8 /ˌvɪdɪəʊ ˈeɪt/ [22] common size and type of magnetic tape cassette used in camcorders

video-conferencing /ˌvɪdɪəʊˈkɒnfərənsɪŋ/ [28] communications service which uses the transmission of video signals through the telephone network to allow groups of people in different locations to have discussions with each other

videophone /ˈvɪdɪəʊfəʊn/ [28] telephone which transmits video images as well as speech signals over long distances

video recorder /ˈvɪdɪəʊ rɪˌkɔːdə(r)/ [1, 21] *see* video cassette recorder

videotex /ˈvɪdɪəʊteks/ [28] viewdata

viewdata /ˈvjuːdeɪtə/ [28] interactive communications service which uses the public telephone network for the transmission of pages of general information in the form of text and graphics for display on a television screen or viewdata terminal

viewdata terminal /ˈvjuːdeɪtə ˌtɜːmɪnəl/ [28] device consisting of a CRT screen and keyboard which is used for receiving and transmitting viewdata communications

vinyl /ˈvaɪnəl/ [16, 17] polyvinyl: plastic material used in making audio records

VLF /ˌviː el ˈef/ [10] very low frequency: frequency between 3kHz and 30kHz

VLSI /ˌviː el es ˈaɪ/ [23] very large scale integration: between 10^3 and 10^4 active components contained on one IC chip

volt /vɒlt/ [4] unit of voltage (V)

voltage /ˈvɒltɪdʒ/ [1] measure of electronic force (measured in volts, V)

voltage drop /ˈvɒltɪdʒ drɒp/ [9] difference in voltage between two points in a circuit

voltage gain /ˈvɒltɪdʒ geɪn/ [11] voltage amplification: comparison of the magnitude of the output voltage of an amplifier with the magnitude of its input voltage

voltmeter /ˈvɒltˌmiːtə(r)/ [5, 19] electronic instrument for measuring electrical voltage

volume /ˈvɒljuːm/ [1] level of sound

volume control /ˈvɒljuːm kənˌtrəʊl/ [13] control for adjusting the loudness of an audio signal

VU meter /ˌviː ˈjuː ˌmiːtə(r)/ [6] volume-unit meter: electronic meter for measuring the power level of an audio signal

Walkman /ˈwɔːkmən/ [5] trade name of a popular type of personal stereo cassette player

waveguide /ˈweɪvgaɪd/ [26, 28] metal duct for guiding microwave signals

wavemeter /ˈweɪvˌmiːtə(r)/ [15] electronic instrument for measuring the frequency of a transmitted signal

window foil /ˈwɪndəʊ fɔɪl/ [9] thin metal tape used in alarm systems to detect the breaking of a glass window

wiper /ˈwaɪpə(r)/ [1] moving contact in a variable component such as a potentiometer or variable resistor

wireless /ˈwaɪələs/ *see* radio (set)

woofer /ˈwʊfə(r)/ [13] large loudspeaker used for low frequency audio signals

workmate /ˈwɜːkmeɪt/ [25] person with whom you work

work placement /ˈwɜːk ˌpleɪsmənt/ [25] relevant job experience as part of training

workshop /ˈwɜːkʃɒp/ [25] building where things are repaired

X-amplifier /ˈeks ˌæmplɪfaɪə(r)/ [19] electronic circuit for increasing the signal controlling the horizontal movement of the electron beam in a cathode ray tube

X-plates /ˈeks pleɪts/ [19] pair of metal plates in a cathode ray tube which use voltages to deflect the electron beam horizontally

Y-amplifier /ˈwaɪ ˌæmplɪfaɪə(r)/ [19] electronic circuit for increasing the signal controlling the vertical movement of the electron beam in a cathode ray tube

Y-plates /ˈwaɪ pleɪts/ [19] pair of metal plates in a cathode ray tube which use voltages to deflect the electron beam vertically

zener diode /ˌziːnə ˈdaɪəʊd/ [4, 5] semiconductor diode which works in reverse bias and is normally used to stabilize a voltage

Zener effect, the /ðə ˈziːnər ɪˌfekt/ [18] sudden increase in the reverse current of a diode at the zener breakdown voltage

zener voltage /ˌziːnə ˈvɒltɪdʒ/ [4] reverse breakdown voltage of a diode at which the zener effect begins

µA /ˈmaɪkrəʊæmp/ [18, 23] microamp (millionth of an amp)

µW /ˈmaɪkrəʊwɒt/ [23] microwatt (millionth of a watt)

Appendix 2
Circuit symbols

Notes

1 A number of variations of circuit symbols are commonly found. For example, —⋀⋁⋀— is still often used although it is no longer the international symbol for a resistor.

2 Some symbol details are often left out in circuit diagrams. For example, the 'a' and 'k' labels and the circle on diodes are not always shown.

Component	Common symbols			
1 fixed resistor	⊏▭⊐	or	—⋀⋁⋀—	
2 variable resistor	▭	or	▭	or ⋀⋁⋀ or ⋀⋁⋀
3 potentiometer	▭	or	⋀⋁⋀	
4 thermistor	▭ −t°	or	⋀⋁⋀ −t°	
5 LDR	⊖	or	⊂⋙⊃	

6 capacitor	⊣⊢ or ⊣(	⊣⊩+	⊣⊬
	fixed	electrolytic	variable
7 inductor	—⟞⟠⟠⟠⟞— or —⟠⟠—	⟠⟠⟠⟠ dust cored	⟠⟠⟠⟠ iron cored
	air cored		
8 transformer	⊰⊱ or ⊰⊱	⊰∥⊱	⊰∥∥∥⊱
	air cored	dust cored	iron cored